What people are say

People of the Outside

Lee Morgan is a timeless modern prophet who evokes stunning and powerful beauty with this awe-inspiring poetry and prose. When I read the writing of Lee Morgan I am seen and I See. One of the greatest and most artful voices of contemporary Craft.
Fio Gede Parma, initiate, mentor, cunning person, and author

Morgan exhibits a puckish pleasure in crafting an interior world for the reader to cross into while hedge-riding his language, so that they may immerse themselves within the crucible of embodied knowing. It is no small feat to write from within the place one desires to occupy; it is a singular and distinguished mark of an artist, and an artist Morgan certainly is.
Sasha Ravitch, author and astrologer

People of the Outside

Witchcraft, Cannibalism, and the Elder Folk

People of the Outside

Witchcraft, Cannibalism, and the Elder Folk

Lee Morgan

MOON BOOKS

Winchester, UK
Washington, USA

JOHN HUNT PUBLISHING

First published by Moon Books, 2024
Moon Books is an imprint of John Hunt Publishing Ltd., No. 3 East Street, Alresford
Hampshire SO24 9EE, UK
office@jhpbooks.net
www.johnhuntpublishing.com
www.moon-books.net

For distributor details and how to order please visit the 'Ordering' section on our website.

Text copyright: Lee Morgan 2023

ISBN: 978 1 80341 521 5
978 1 80341 539 0 (ebook)
Library of Congress Control Number: 2023935063

A CIP catalogue record for this book is available from the British Library.

Design: Lapiz Digital Services

UK: Printed and bound by CPI Group (UK) Ltd, Croydon, CR0 4YY
Printed in North America by CPI GPS partners

We operate a distinctive and ethical publishing philosophy in all areas of our business, from our global network of authors to production and worldwide distribution.

Contents

Also by Lee Morgan

A Deed Without a Name
Unearthing the History of Traditional Witchcraft
ISBN:1780995490

Standing and Not Falling
A Sorcerous Primer in Thirteen Moons
ISBN: 1789040140

Sounds of Infinity
Traditional Witchcraft and the Faerie Faith
ISBN: 1881098540

Wooing the Echo
Book One of the Christopher Penrose Novels
ISBN: 1780998961

The Bones Would Do
Book Two of the Christopher Penrose Novels
ISBN: 1782798714

The Gusty Deep
ISBN: 1608642216

This book was written on kunanyi, muwinina country — it always was, and always will be. This land was never ceded.

Foreword

by Sasha Ravitch

Those who have been privileged with the sensorium-melting experience of reading Lee Morgan's books — both his charming fiction as well as his immensely popular explorations of witchcraft — have already been initiated into the ecstasy of his language. With preternatural grace, he expertly weaves together eloquence and accessibility, poetic finesse and acute candour, hypnotising imagery and cunning praxis, and leaves one both furiously enraptured and mesmerised in the process. There is a great legacy of writers within the Western canon who seek to facilitate experience through their work: Jacques Derrida applied his deconstructive tools to the language in *Of Grammatology* as a way of exhibiting the deconstructive method, and J.G. Ballard swerved the structure of language into sentence-long pile-ups in his novel *Crash*.

Morgan exhibits a puckish pleasure in crafting an interior world for the reader to cross into while hedge-riding his language, so that they may immerse themselves within the crucible of embodied knowing. It is no small feat to write from within the place one desires to occupy; it is a singular and distinguished mark of an artist, and an artist Morgan certainly is. *People of the Outside* takes an enormous risk in giving a shape and form — teeth and claws — to nascent sensations and dark-of-the-night thoughts many of us have quieted away, kept secret and safe from the Over-Culture's disparaging fluorescent lights of judgement. But what enlivens that throbbing red serpent, what makes it grow fat and wet with the pulse of the thing, comes alive within the pages of this new work: as bold and subversive, perhaps, as it is brazenly relaxed.

Cannibalism is inseparable, inextricable from, and mutually inclusive with Witchcraft, and those who endeavour to sever the two only exsanguinates the hallowed symphony of blood-and-bone-memory the Witch carries in their twisted veins. While historical documents, papers of inquisitorial interrogation, reports from this and that witchfinder general, and legends and lore have no problem reminding us of the cannibalising nature of the Witch, it does appear that the modern revival of interest and, perhaps even romanticisation of the Witch, has erased from her a certain monstrosity — erased her appetite. Morgan adroitly reminds us of the discomfiting truth of our origin stories — from Neanderthal to Denisovan, from Cagot to Christian. Within these pages we are linked, by large intestine and cerebral cortex, to our "unclean conspirators", and subsequently find ourselves answering in daylight the questions we ask ourselves in the dark.

He does not choose to focus on solely one region, but guides us on a journey through European and Basque witches, the Benandanti and Malandanti of Italy, the Hungarian Taltos, the Aboriginal Spirit Doctor, the Phi Krahang and Krasue of Thailand, and so much more. One begins to recognise the vast sea of immeasurable interconnectivity we share with the Elder Folk and their descendants — these qualities mythologised in our folklore, but still active in our culture. The profound vastness of sympathetic folklore regarding witches, even as it expands across the tremendous arc of the earth, helps situate the reader and witch within the context of a greater ancestral inheritance, and a legacy one is best integrating instead of rejecting. Honest integration: a courageous and authentic acknowledgement, incorporation, and even direct invitation, this is exactly what Morgan asks of us.

Beyond the generous amount of anthropological, genetic, and folkloric research Morgan provides, he pivotally challenges the reader to recognise the Elder Folk's reddened imprint in their genetic memory. Why should we not invite the cannibal within to break (sweet)bread with us? This is an alien gift but a gift nonetheless: our own mini-initiatory cauldron to roil in as we scry cannibalism's state of interiority for Sapiens. Where we are pushed to recognise the ways in which we actively, even if unconsciously, self-cannibalise the Elder Folk within us. Suspended and sundered, we are caught in the crosshairs of contradiction: desire and disgust as both what churns the scarlet waters of the witch-blood, while simultaneously wrecking us against its cliffs.

While he never explicitly refers to it by name, we are absolutely directed toward acute analysis of our neglected projective identification. For those unfamiliar, projective identification was coined by psychoanalyst Melanie Klein, student of Freud, in her specialised research on the psychopathology of children. Klein recognised many things which popular society around her wished to reject (similar to her mentor), such as the innate homicidal impulse within children. But most useful and immensely applicable within the context of this work, and the proffered rejection of the Elder Folk within us, is this particular Kleinian theory. Klein posited that we, indoctrinated by the rules and mores of "civil society", develop deep and masterfully complex pathological processes in order to protect ourselves from the truly "amoral" or "evil" parts of ourselves; to confront that we had desires, thoughts, impulses which violated the social contract would be like ego-annihilation, and subsequently, must be avoided at all cost. But we have to put those very bad feelings somewhere, because the longer they are within us, even unconsciously possessed, the greater our sense of dread that we are "bad, wrong, and evil".

People love to offload the things they don't want any more onto others, and that is what we do with all our "bad" desires, impulses, and thoughts, as well. We project them into another person (or peoples), and for one blissful moment, we are emptied of our fears that we are the bad guy, because we are certain the Other is the bad guy. But alas, there is a greater issue here: we still (unconsciously) identify that those projected identities are ours. This portends a more sickening discomfort, as we feel empty of what was intrinsically ours, and paranoid that the other person will harm us with ourselves. This often goes in one of two directions: we attempt to punish the other person for representing and reminding us of our horrible outsourced qualities, ultimately leading to the termination of the relationship, or, at best, it allows us to have a moment of awakening wherein we recognise that these are our horrible qualities and that we must find a way to integrate and reconcile with them.

It becomes imminently clear throughout *People of the Outside* how this trick of projective identification plays a treacherous role in divorcing ourselves from, well, ourselves — and the significant cost this disintegration has taken on intersectionality marginalised people. While we return time and time again to the role of the cannibal, Morgan also explores the ways in which the Other, itself, both becomes, and is inborn, as the Witch within the popular imagination. He is thorough in his exploration of the demonic Other, whether the moniker of Witch is attributed via neurodivergence, gender identity and sexuality, race and ethnicity, the immense stigma around menstruating people, a societal contempt for women, and even different religions. He takes a risk in sharing what he does, as it is an act of courage to hold a mirror up to Sapiens — so prone to avoiding the truth in ourselves — while asking us to introject, swallow whole, the monstrosity of both our spirit-selves and our psyche-pathology. The Witch as abject, as abomination, and that-which-transgresses has been replaced by a sanitised, digestible, costume in the 21st century in ways few of our ancestors could have ever suspected.

That beautiful 'dark continent' of the Witch's body, as Hélène Cixous coined it, has become a technicolor spectacle.

But when we investigate closely, it is not the Witch which has become marketable, an object of desire, but rather some strange claw-less imago. For how can anything pleasing or consumable truly be Witch? The Witch, if one looks closer, is still that which society recoils from: the figure who forces our defensive projections, who makes a shrill cathexis in our unconscious cauldron, conjuring a fear (that we might, ourselves, become that dreaded other thing) that becomes hatred. In an attempt to make the Witch a palatable good-object, a performative costume, it has been turned only into an image — divorced of the blood-lusting, power-churning, anti-human force which it has always been. But the feelings reserved for the Witch still exist, and they are found within the grossular alembic of the Over-Culture's coupled disgust and fear of aberration from the narrow margin of "normal". That is as unchanging in the 21st century as it was in the 16th century, as it was in the 12th century.

While reading the advanced copy of this book, I attended our local opera house's performance of Englebert Humperdinck's *Hansel & Gretel*. The spirits which populate the pastoral of witchcraft are prone to blending the margins of our mundane with synchronicities simply too visceral to reject, and so, too, became my experience at the opera. When the Witch was revealed, I was struck by the casting choice: the singular person of colour in an entirely white cast, a man who would spend the entirety of the performance wearing a costume inspired by drag queens during Mardi Gras. It is not unusual in opera for genders to be swapped, of course, but within the context of reading Morgan's work, I could not avoid the slow climb of goosebumps as I sat with the casting choice of the Witch as a black man in drag (replete with sequins and pink bouffant wig), singing with an intentionally comically feminine affect. When Hansel and Gretel trick the Witch into her own oven and she's proclaimed dead, the entire audience — children and adults alike — launched into raucous applause and cheers — going as far as to stand up from their seats, shouting their celebration of her death. While the Witch was boo-ed for her cannibalism, the audience laughed when the townsfolk, in turn, cannibalised the Witch.

The unconscious casting and design choices for the Witch, and the collective response of the audience, proved a corroborative nod to the prescience of Morgan's observations. *People of the Outside* is a challenging work. I would argue that all texts on witchcraft should, in fact, be challenging works, as witchcraft and the role of the Witch are by their very virtue adversarial. We should not feel comfortable, we should not be made to feel safe when we find ourselves at the nexus of the crossroad, or at the threshold of the hedge. If we disavow part of who we are, then all of who we are remains a stranger to us, and that is where the truest danger lies — a fear of oneself, a fear of the Other as it exists at all times within Us. My sense is that this work will become increasingly relevant as time unwinds its crooked path before us (and behind us), and more and more details about the Elder Folk become clarified — both through the advances in genetic science, and through other avenues of knowing.

When one reads what Morgan posits, the heavy, felt-sense, viscosity of knowing sits like the forbidden flesh in the pit of the stomach. There is the signature nausea, the thread of rejection, but the implicit recognition of something nearly-forgotten whispering first in the fetch before stirring up the blood. We owe Morgan a debt of gratitude for the courage and the consistency with which he tenderly regards what is subversive in our nature — the rejected hiding in plain sight, the Elder-Folk in the room. We owe him a debt of gratitude for the research he compiled, and the honesty of his self-reflection. We owe him a debt of gratitude for encouraging, granting a sort of permission, for us to fall in love with the blood and bone memory of what makes us Other to begin with — why we find ourselves hissing into chalices and shapeshifting through the eye of a needle. Never to be cut off above the breath again, we demand — and so we must recognise the legacy from which we descend. Morgan illustrates that legacy, and connects those amongst us called Witch back to our long-toothed antecedents of yore. May your family reunion be an ecstatic one.

Happy Feasting,
Sasha Ravitch

Chapter 1

What Sews a Witchcraft from a Baby Hide?

Witchcraft owned your skin before you ever thought you did. You slipped on into it down the drain-pipe of a birth cord and witchcraft had you sewn into the flesh-purse of your baby hide. You absorbed her along the ancestor life-from-death cord, and she made you a little alien. People make words up for things. People like to hedge things in and around with noises. They made the word 'witch', using different sounds in multiple noise-making systems, as they wandered through our uncanny valley. A smattering of poetry, a series of key taboos that work like a key to a mystery-lock in a highly visible, and therefore largely invisible, back-to-front door between your legs. People will talk about what makes a witchcraft, what makes a witch, which stitch sews in a witch to our blood knowing? How many eyes do we have when all are considered? Some of the answers to these crooked riddles will have value, at some level. Only at the level of the gaze. Words are an extension of the gaze, sticking everything to the look of itself. Regardless of the appearance of our human mother we all slipped out of the cunny of a ghost-woman with the hair of the Neanderthals on her chin. Yet words for all their battering never did stretch around the slick sensation of drawing out the liquid essence of the fetch bones, your back and ribs cracking into a new shape as you prepare for flight. Words never did define the difference between the quick and the dead in the moment where you show The Devil you're brave, and canny, and too twisted for the straight or the narrow... The moment the show him the back of your neck and open your skull-door for the darkest and brightest of adventures.

We cannot define the slippery edges of an horrendous transformation into the stuff of nightmare and dream, and worst of all the middle seam that sticks them to each other in a slow, gelatinous gleam. But we can dance with it. We can fuck it, and kiss it, until it is known to us in the biblical sense. Then when we speak about it well enough, when we undress its history in the strange language of thorn-sharp reason, and the other type of rose-like reason we call instinct, we will find echoes of the third path of witching-reason behind those words. But never in front of them. I was there when the books I write became haunted, yet I did not make them haunted. I was made to get out of the way of the birthing labours of the foremother who grew hair on her chin and whose teeth were somewhat longer than my own. So, welcome to what is left. A hearth inside a cave. It's a cave not because the story is primitive, but simply because it is empty, a place the wind makes its music through, much like a hollow bone. What you will read here is a book about being strange. It's a book about being a little alien. Through the use of the thorns and the flowers it will wear away at the tangled binding threads, trying to feel how deeply placed they are. It will take us all to an encounter with the monstrous, in whose reflection we might see ourselves.

For the first time in history this is possible. This is no small thing. A witch's voice cracking out into the primary narrative, making them tremble...

Chapter 2

What in the Dark They Fear We Witches Do

There is a stranger at the door, the smoke hole or the window. Our forebears understood this enough to feel fear. They were the People of the Outside, after all, cultural-bearers of everything rejected. Yet they are also someone from within. They've been at your fireside and chuckled with you about the behaviour of geese and children. It is not clear if they are a someone, or a something, this well-known stranger. Though by their nature you can never pick it when you meet them. They seem like an ordinary reddened human being. They even bleed that colour when you cut them above the breath to steal their witch-blood.

Judging from their hidden character they should be of the outside. They resonate with the outsider qualities of the wild, they have the fox's eyes of cold fire, they should be exiled, and yet in some form they usually reside inside the human community. Often this Other is not defined as fully human, despite being as familiar as your aunty and carrying out normal daily tasks. Their existence seems like a kind of betrayal of all this normality. Though they likely can't help it, their night function, when paired with those other mundane bonds is part of the horror, the lingering fear of predation from a trusted familiar. That feeling when someone saw the otherwise respectable Goody Procter with the devil...

Until recently the voice on this topic has belonged to the accuser and we have not yet fully appreciated the luxury of our new voice. Not at a truly historical level anyway. The voice is now given to the one who would have been cut above the breath in the past, rather than only handed only to the cutter. The voice is now with shared even with the one who often, if not always, acts in favour of the more-than-human over the human. Though witches are capable of taking away ills from humans, they generally do this by transferring the problem elsewhere. Their voice, our voice, is defined by some simply as the opposite to the belief of the mainstream. Whether the mainstream are Christians or Atheists their opposite principle changes from fearsome devil worshipper to irrational idiot.

This is probably because most of humanity seems to find it easier to think in twos rather than threes or anything higher, let alone to be able to flexibly move around between different possibilities based on context. Gaining a voice allows us to talk back and contaminate discourse with our cunning perspective. It allows us to engage in the discourse of our age. It allows us to challenge the dominant forms of social engagement with something from the Outside.

I use a certain amount of reason in this book naturally, or perhaps sometimes it uses me. Research, that process of digging into the archeology of written things, requires it. Yet there are different forms of reasoning available to the witch, different ways of feeling into things to discern their shape and to sing them into being. There is an accumulative language of symbols, where we build a story through inference, sigil, and dream.

Our heretical gaze and sophisticated habits of thought are imagined from the world inside the boxes to be part of a well-constructed conspiracy, one made up of people in power mingling with those who are not thought to have any power. It is imagined to be physically vaster in scale than it is, this witchcraft of the eyes and brain, probably more so than it's ever been in reality.

In a smaller tribal or village context the accusations and the punishments are more personal, more intimate and perhaps therefore more terrible. The intimate quality of the initial betrayal engenders this violence from the inside. It is not uncommon for there to be one or two people who are not as they appear, who are People of the Outside, capable of working against the day-lit, cohesive values of the group, possibly even whilst upholding those values in other contexts and other actions.

There are two popular ways to explain the paranoia that lies behind this almost universal happening. It could be a form of neurosis that seems to be so central to Sapiens that it exists the world over. If it is not a mental illness, some intrinsic perversity of this species, it must connect us to a common experience in humans. There is also a dark, hidden heart present both in the practice of witchcraft and the intrinsic fear of it, a third option that partakes of both of the others and may be integral to Sapiens as a species. What then is this history that is at once comprised of a forgotten event, a neurosis. and a reality?

To add yet another dimension to this tale it might even be the case that how efficiently a culture finds ways to integrate and sublimate divergent individuals, and to manage the fear of the insider-outsider relationship determines how long and how well that culture continues to thrive, and how long before they begin dunking one another in water to determine guilt or innocence. If we look closer at these Othered individuals, or clusters in some cases (as numerous divergent conditions pass to children in the blood), we discover a basis in fear of this scapegoat population, a fear they may somehow, just through dreaming it, have an underhanded way to push back against established power stories.

Around the world these People of the Outside are very often, but far from always, women, and the reason why from a purely social perspective seems obvious. Women possess the enormous power of birth-giving, and yet are most often smaller and less physically powerful as individual bodies, they also possess the uncanny blood that flows with the moon. Menstrual blood is so often strictly tabooed in cultures all around the world, to the extent of some rules providing for women to have to stay down wind rather than up wind of the other people, that one questions if these practices take us all the way to the door of the most primordial taboos of Sapiens? And if those taboos are potentially that old, what is the forgotten story behind their early and pre-emptive violence of this plot-line?

There is this sense that when our species represses or sanctions a group or a practice that inevitably do so through a repression of the qualities we identify in them inside ourselves as well. Not only must the characteristics of the oppressed be repressed in ourselves, but also the humanity of the Other, like the witch they are no longer a full person but a monster, they must somehow be storied as uncanny, even if it requires stories with no basis in reality. Here we find the narratives of explanation in myth that help to explain why that group is treated differently, what damaging effects will occur if the tradition of persecuting them is neglected, and why this tradition is crucial to the upholding of all order and decency.

If you neglect the persecution of the half-blind widow then it will only be so long before rampant animal sodomy will overtake the land. This may help the pro-social animal Sapiens to block out the inevitable guilt they will feel when punishing the said widow. This line of thinking will continue up until contemporary times where some people still believe that marrying another adult human should be compared to marrying bridges or dogs. These aggressive stories also help to work away at the resentment that an oppressed group, or person, is likely to feel towards those in the privileged group. It's harder to hate the oppressor when you've been fed the story you are inherently a monster from the first taste of your mother's milk. As a born member of the Othered group you will be expected to repress or internalise the aggression of that story, turning it inward as shame, or even masochistic identification with the oppressor, if no other ritual outlets are available to you. All too often such narratives end in self-deletion by that Person of the Outside.

It is arguable that this violence comes into play whenever humans kill anything or use literal violence to oppress others, whether human or non-human animals. There is mental work required both for the aggressor and the victim, repressions and delusions, self-trickery and sublimated sadism enter a heady soup in the cauldron of humankind… So it is little wonder this bubbling mess creates a plethora of psychic phenomenon that are tossed up in a way that seems almost random. To put it another way, there is little wonder to it, as our breed of witches and nightmares gurgles away from sight in the blackness of the lower gut.

Humanity's Other, this one that so worries people they fill their homes with charms against it, walks with us through every part of the world we have ventured. Some cultures are better at expiating our alien-style inheritance in cathartic rituals that often involve seeming punishments of self or others. There is always this internal struggle, perhaps typical of us as a hybrid still evolving into its most effective fusion-form.

On average our species has quite highly developed empathy even when compared to other animals, many of whom still rival us.[1] It is an empathy capable of walking hand-in-hand with an almost equal need for catharsis through savagery and scapegoating, anyone who has taken in even a casual sense of the history of the species could not deny either of these facts. Luckily we are mercurial or it would be easy to give up on us. It is fair to say though that part of the sensations of solidarity and tribalism spring from being united in hatred for outsiders or a specific enemy.

We are very intelligent animals, yet almost entirely blind to the sources of that drive and control our behaviour simply because we are so wrapped up in them. The familiar has always been terribly unfamiliar to us. This is why hearing from our more often rejected minorities is a new opportunity for our species.

We are hearing the voices of witches, of queer people, trans people, neuro-divergent people and some of us, like myself, who are all of these things, and some unnamed ones also. As a species we play out the fate-loops of insider and outsider in this way for survival and reproduction in such an unconscious way that it can appear we are often strangers to emotional reason.

One part of Sapiens satiates itself on the group cohesion created by the stress of shared hatred, shared self-righteousness, and other people's confirmation that one is indeed virtuous and caring. The other parts of ourselves, like the socialised self, have to turn their eyes away from the implications of our lifestyles. The modern psyche therefore has perhaps the greatest gulf between the socialised-self and the Othered impulses. We project all that when we point the finger at our witch, our scapegoat, our heretic, our diseases, our terror. This is dangerous as it makes the return of the darkness more unpredictable.

Whilst we tend to look down on societies and call them primitive when they hold sacrificial and expiation rituals they might actually have more emotional intelligence and realism, one built up over generations. When it comes to understanding sublimation, and how to trigger release in the human limbic system, their intelligence might far surpass our own. Without this crucial skill there is likely to be some far worse result later. Instead of simply opposing religion our world will need to learn how to think in layers, to use both the insider and the outsider parts of the self at the same time.

When people are crushed to death in frenzies during soccer matches we see that this primal instinct of tribal connection and blood-letting is still entirely present in modern people. No doubt this is why something which is merely a game is treated with such reverence as sport is by Sapiens. It is such a simple interaction that every so-called race in our whole genetic diversity-lacking species relates to chasing balls and trying to get somewhere very fast.

This distance between our primal impulses and our socialisation isn't unique to humans, however. Here I will provide a poignant example the uneasy feeling given off by a tale of murder that arises from an Orangutang who lost his mother and was raised by humans. Unlike the rather emotionally sophisticated cage rats this primate behaves far more like the worst of Sapiens.

> *Sugito was staring off into space with a funny look that I had never seen before. He studiously avoided looking in Doe's (foster sister) direction. After some time… he slowly approached. He held her under the water until she stopped fighting. Then, standing on two legs, he raised both arms over his head and brought them down, fluttering, in front of him [like] a shaman… performing rituals of obsequiousness to his god… Sugito knew perfectly well that Doe was dead. He had killed her.[2]*

There is something naked about this account. The simplicity of the words make you feel as it has watched the elicit murder of a Sapien. Probably also because the behaviour sounds eerily familiar. We will never know what (beyond perhaps a perceived flickering of the perverse in Sugito, a curiosity about destruction) drove him. But when we read this we must recognise, given that Orangutangs who are mothered in the wild seldom murder, that this impulse and this process of dehumanising the victim exists overtly in Sapiens too. The way Sugito needed to look away and couldn't look into her face, could not share the open door of his gaze with her, is a simple form of converting Doe from a fellow Orangutang-person into a witch.

This act of looking away, of denying the sticky, psychic interaction of the gaze, and the strange ritualised behaviour Sugito followed with, comes from the same root as the stories Sapiens have told about witches, Jewish people, or the queer.

Elicit, pointless, murder from within the group of this sort is highly socialised against in most human societies, yet it can in some places still be called gay panic if there is existing monsterisation built up around the victim.

The gay and trans panic defences are examples of why Sapiens usually needs to invent stories to justify the need to commit a perverse and anti-social act, especially on repeat. And, of course, as a creature with intact second level intentionality we know that others likely think as we think, and feel similarly to how we feel, therefore for all but the most sociopathic, guilt must be defended against via stories that monsterise.

For people who share a magical worldview, including the major world religions, it is an easy step to consider that such tendencies as exist in Sapiens, when repressed from expression might then be spiritually weaponised. This paranoia of the gaze lives in us as well as Sugito. That fear that someone who was looking at you judgmentally might in fact be looking balefully, that they might have subtly brought you misfortune with their evil eye, is a very widespread human concern. Perhaps it is even one of the core entirely Sapien beliefs. Furthermore, accusing someone of such a largely unprovable crime against you gives license to carrying out punishments that allows the expression of repressed sadism, and perhaps even internal self-hatred for all of our own personal, hidden, Otherwise characteristics.

Let us talk about those marks of the Other...

One of the earlier accounts of a witchcraft we would recognise is from The Books of Samuel (600-500BCE).[3] Here we meet the Witch of Endor, she is a woman, her art of raising the dead is forbidden. With necromancy she conjures the deceased from a pagan netherworld from which they rise, and we know she has The Sight, because no one else present can either see or hear the ghost. Despite this, after the encounter Saul collapses in terror and is so worn down by being in the presence of the dead that the witch, who is herself not impacted, kills a fatted calf to restore his vitality.

In the Yalkut of Judaic tradition it is asserted that whilst the querent can't see the ghost they can hear them, and the necromancer themselves can see them but not hear them. In these traditions we find the witch as an interactive go-between with the querent and the Underworld who is not depleted in the presence of these powers, and whose art is already forbidden in her culture. Whatever that force is that rises from the earth as both plural, Elohim meaning gods, who she describes as rising as a singular. This may tell us something about the deeper structure of her way of thinking. Naturally though the biblical emphasis is not on her.

A detailed written accounts of familiar witchcraft beliefs in Rome also appears in *The Golden Ass* by Apuleius[4] (125-185 CA). Here we see a couple of witches, one old and leathery the other described as attractive, both are highly sexual and adulterous and dishonest, they are closer to their animal nature, with transformation and flight as a bird through the means of an ointment. Even as early as this there is mention of witches cannibalising human flesh from corpses, and the taking of human body parts for their spells. Witchcraft seems to be entirely related to women, as Medea, Meroe, and Pamphile are the only witches mentioned.

Despite this fact it can clearly be contracted by men, as the ointment for transformation and flying still works when rubbed on a man's body, causing him to transform into an animal, just as the women do. It's hard to know whether the story as a whole should be read as a half ironic or semi-serious treatise against the dangers of women. Either way it is clear that witchcraft seems to rest primarily in the hands of women, but is highly contagious.

Apuleius was a Berber of Nubian extract educated in a Roman style, though it is noteworthy that he himself was accused of bewitching the rich widow he married.[5] Whether writing about witchcraft was so contagious it caused this belief or whether it had some basis in fact is unknown. Here the enemy within the gates is distinctly womanly in nature and has a lot to do with the lure of sexual temptation, which men seem curiously helpless in the grip of. Nonetheless, a very evident cruelty is perceivable in the actions of women, along with a sense of a secret inversion of the overt power structure, one that even leads to them actively pissing on men.

The story seems to tell us that whilst men might believe they are in charge, underneath this surface illusion arcane powers are allowing women to pull all the real strings. Apuleius seems kind of cheerfully resigned about this fact, but nonetheless records the recognisable tropes of what will later erupt into full scale witchcraft hysteria in the future. What he is good-humoured about the future will put into a thumbscrew. If we cast our gaze on what witches would later be accused of we find them to be a kind of elaboration on themes that were already established centuries before of the beginning of the common era.

Whilst the accusations would become more detailed in the future one would be surprised if Apuleius was not drawing from a well-fleshed-out source of folk knowledge. Sorcery of the necromantic, Underworldly nature was already banned in some places hundreds of years before Christianity emerged. The most common later accusations we will explore below (other than the obvious one of maleficium or harmful magic) are: possessing an ointment that can help witches to fly, the profane kiss, turning into beasts, cannibalism — often of baby flesh — women as the perverse mother figure who kills her child or performs abortions or possesses a beard, feeding an imp from a secret teat even if a man, hagging as the classical nightmare riding astride the victim, sexual perversions including incest and sodomy practiced by both sexes, and vampire-like life force theft of men's virility.

The witch's behaviour represented a complete inversion of the life way of the culture making the accusation, a world turned upside down, and all major taboos violated. We don't hear much about paedophilic behaviour among witches, the absence of which perhaps speaks loudly in and of itself. This may all sound a bit obvious until we really think about it. Because it is at once both created by a shared, hybrid, form of mental life, and also something that becomes nothing less than utterly true. It is a truth that makes you wonder if the accusation of witchcraft itself forms a primordial human release valve, existing as much for the explanation of People from the Outside as it does for a channelling of the perverse joy of persecution?

If, much like the Orangutang murder by Sugito, the witchcraft accusation allows a strange curiosity to be sated in Sapiens? For people to enjoy the salacious entertainment of dark and forbidden activities that excite strong feelings of disgust and horror? The thrill of horror and pity are known to be the cornerstone of the tragic genre after all. When we watch horror play out on a stage or screen we can safely identify with the blood-shed and struggle of the characters.

Through the real-life-story of witchcraft people could exercise their own Othered, sexual, and cannibalistically predatorily fantasies, fantasies that might consist of epigenetic or ancestral memories of times in the past where our forebears were performing, or forced to perform, these taboos. The accusation of witchcraft came to seem a safe way to project those feelings onto an Other — safe at least until someone turns a gaze on another, until someone points a real finger, or a bone.

Witches and destructive sorcerers, often cannibalistic ones, haunt the consciousness of most Sapien societies. It is kind of obvious, almost too obvious maybe, to mention the lack of scientific explanations in the past for the workings of nature, the ones we may now tell ourselves we have the true explanation for. The smaller number of witch terrors in post-industrial cultures may be due to greater safety, higher living standards and life-expectancy. Despite these seeming improvement other scapegoats are still found. We are not without our state-sanctioned bogeymen, whether they be religiously extreme Islamic sects, communism, Satanic Panics, supposed homosexual agendas, or conspiracy theories that in some circles take the place of the witch. In other circles the witch continues in the place of the witch.

Today the current theories of evil in English-speaking countries focus a lot on pedophiles, that group who are interestingly absent from the earlier church-led accusations against witches. Perhaps stranger than the fact scapegoating and fear of hidden evil still exists in our post-scientific world is the fact that the very things witches are accused of (I say are, rather than were, because there are a number of countries where witchcraft killings are still current) were once thrown by Rome at early Christians. It is strange for its precision as much as its lurid quality that we find many of these same tropes applied by Roman pagans to their new competitor religion.

Though we don't find night-flight, ointments, or animal transformation in the mix we do find worship of the sex organ of the male leader 'as if he were their father' (not quite sure what they meant by that), incest, bisexual sex, sex between elderly and younger people, incest — otherwise described as indiscriminate sex — followed by cannibalistic feasts on sacrificed dead babies.[6] It is significant to note that this cannibalistic feast supposedly happened after the light was put out by the involuntary actions of a tied up dog. This is significant because like Sugito during his orangutang murder, it denies the possibility for a witnessing gaze.

The indiscriminate orgiastic rite happens in darkness with lamps out, like many of the Greek mystery traditions, where none may see with whom they are intimate and the putting out of the light is something that they do not take responsibility for. The light is extinguished by the will of a type of beast given little social merit in that culture. The language of what these early Christian heretics were being accused of is very clear, they are putting out the light of reason and decency, denying the holy gaze which affirms our appearance in the eyes of others, and doing it with the will of the dog within themselves.

Everything deemed unclean by Roman pagan society is connected with the canine and it is easy to see why. The domestication of the dog likely followed the same format as that of dingoes in Australia, where one could speak of wild dingoes and 'camp dingoes', who were still partially wild but went back and forth between the human and the wild. This going back and forth likely impacted people with a sense that they were a crossing-over animal, one who was involved somehow in protecting and guiding humans when they passed out of the camp, away from the fire, and out into the wild zone of the ancestors into what we now call death.

The early Christians who refused their social duties to the state, and therefore threatened its integrity. Jews, various heretics, Templars, and even lepers have also been accused of many of these things, as Carlo Ginsberg showed.[7] Even things like the profane kiss on the arse was not only ascribed to the devil and the witch but to the Waldenses, Templars, Bogomils, and the Cathars who were all accused of variants of the 'the kiss of shame'[8] which is associated by the accusing cultures with ritual uncleanliness.

We will return later to this notion of ritual cleanliness and uncleanliness, and the ways that the breaking of this sense of order interrupts the gaze, time itself, and creates the discord of devil's acres from which phantoms begin to emerge.

Notes

1. In an experiment with rats it has been shown that a rat will free another rat from an uncomfortable trap, even if it doesn't know that rat, and it will privilege doing this over obtaining its favourite treats. This happens even with cage rats. Cage humans do not always behave like this. Church R. M., Emotional reactions of rats to the pain of others. J. Comp. Physiol. Psychol. 52, 132 (1959).

2. B.M.F Galdikas, National Geographic-157 (1980) p.832.

3. English Standard Version Bible, 1 Samuel 28. (2001). ESV Online. https://esv.literalword.com/

4. Apuleius; Ellen D Finkelpearl. (Trans.) (2021) *The Golden Ass* (edited and abridged by Peter Singer). New York: Liveright Publishing Corporation; London.

5. The *Golden Ass* (2013). Retrieved 24 December 2021, from https://womeninantiquityblog.wordpress.com/2013/05/13/the-golden-ass/

6. Norman Cohn, *Europe's Inner Demons: The Demonization of Christians in Medieval Christendom.*, University of Chicago Press; Revised ed. edition (2001) pp.23-42.

7. Carlo Ginzburg, *Ecstasies: Deciphering the Witches' Sabbath.*, The University of Chicago Press, (1991) pp.33-63.

8. Lois Martin, *The History Of Witchcraft*, Google Books, 2022, https://books.google.com.au/books Accessed 2 Nov 2022, p.32.

Chapter 3

Witch-Blood and the Beast

Around the world people consider something like witchcraft, or a kind of semi-involuntary malefic sorcerer, to exist as a Person of the Outside. This group of invisible outsiders are on the inside, nonetheless they are thought to have some other type of blood in them beyond standard human blood. They possess witch-blood and are almost a subspecies living among human groups. They might be accused of doing evil magic working against the aims of the group.

Often there is some mythic reason in that culture why certain bloodlines carry this malevolence as a tendency, and whether or not these witches can help what they do or not varies. Usually the story the sorcerers themselves hold can be counted on to be a bit different to the story told about them, but they are seldom asked. Cannibalism, or other sublimated cannibalistic acts, are often central to this story, as what better typifies antisocial behaviour than eating other people? Cannibalism is a very common claim which is associated with Otherwise Folk by many an over-culture. This ranges from the subtle threat that Nicnevan[1] or other folklore witches would come for small children who were naughty, and goes as far as to include colonialist accusations against indigenous peoples in different parts of the world.[2] It's fair to say that as an accusation it packs a punch.

These claims occur over a wide ranging geographical space which we will explore in the chapters below. Before we pursue this I will look at some other taboos to do with ritual uncleanliness. Following on from the way women have been linked to witchcraft I would like to consider the numerous cultures where menstrual blood is a focus for sometimes savage exclusion, exposure of the bleeding woman, and even imprisonment.

Stan Gooch,[3] drawing largely on James Frazer, makes reference to the virulence of multiple Sapien culture's customs and we cannot help looking at the generally strong reaction to menstruating woman as a deep form of Othering. So much is revealed about humanity in our fear of the red river of our bloodlines running down women's legs. We find examples of an almost direct confession of anxiety around the hidden, internal mysteries of reproduction. Among the Aranda, a man admitted to Mircea Eliade[4] the ancestors stole the secrets of magic from women in the form of the bull-roarer and dilly bag. Among the Dogon in Africa it was a blood-marked skirt which allowed men to establish dominion.[5]

In Hoodoo[6] menstrual blood is associated with raw, direct power over men and gives control to the woman over his behaviour if slipped into his food or drink. In some Romani traditions the shadow of the skirt of a bleeding woman should not be cast across a man.[7] Whilst the general message of these practices is that the blood has an ambiguous power, it's clear there is fear and awe mixed into it. The menstruating woman's gaze, or her feet touching the ground, or her blood touching the pathways which men will walk, or her laying upon his bedroll are often avoided, sometimes at pain of death.[8]

There are stories among the Dogon in Central Africa that describe how, (much like the bull-roarer), the men stole a sacred skirt from the women, stained with menstrual blood, and thereby claimed for all time her magical power. This echoes again the feeling we get in Apuleius that witchcraft is contagious, it is catching, and it passes from women unto men. These stories seem to give voice to the uncanny power that women and the menstruating body were deemed to have, and perhaps to explain why it must be ritually controlled. After the theft of the bloodied item all the dances, and songs of power that migrated to the men who must guard against it being re-taken at all costs.

Narratives of this sort seem to suggest traces of mythic spores, settling under history's leaf-loam, forming justifications for the prohibitions faced by menstruating women in many cultures. In some parts of the world we even see a semi-admirable sort of honesty about what is at the root of these concerns. I will use this space to try to quickly summarise the menstrual mythos, where it links with similar ones throughout the world, and the temporary pariah status faced by the bleeding woman. The geographical range some of these stories is broad enough that it promotes a remarkably ancient last-likely-contact date to their substrates.

To the Nunga and Yura of South Australia, the Gadigal of New South Wales, the Yagara of Queensland, the highlanders of Papua New Guinea, and Torres Straight Islanders, menstruating women[9] were thought to risk drying up food supplies by using them whilst bleeding, and can bring down misfortune upon men if she bleeds on the ground of any of the sacred tracks or in some cases drinking from certain water sources. In South and Central Africa there are taboos against menstruating women drinking milk from cattle lest the cattle die, or touching her husband's weapons lest he die in battle. In West Africa she must not touch his food, sit in his seat or lay on his bed, lest he die. The Dravidians of India require separate doors for menstruating women to pass through, she must not walk over common ground, or share paths with other non-bleeders. In parts of North America everything the menstruating woman steps on may die, and if a man walks over a track where she has walked his legs will immediately swell.[10]

Ruth Benedict[11] tells us that among the Kwakiutl the bleeding woman must be veiled to cover her venomous gaze, here we see a link between menstruation and the witch's the evil eye. The Talmud[12] declares ritual uncleanness upon menstruating women in some detail, covering what colours of discharge are pure and impure. In Zoroastrianism Ahura Muzda[13] (their god) declares that menstrual flow is the work of Ahriman their devil. The bleeder is not allowed to eat food to fulfilment as the strength she will accrue would funnel through to unclean demons that are upon her. In Hindu teachings Brahman says that if a man approaches a menstruating woman his strength, eye sight (the evil eye), and wisdom will all fail.[14]

Pliny, a big influencer of European views on the subject, also said that a menstruating woman walking around crops could cause the crops to fail, and may also destroy their parasites.[15] In Loango in Africa a bleeding woman must not touch the ground. Among the Akamba in East Africa if a man walked over somewhere a bleeding woman walked his own partner would become barren. In South Africa among the so called 'Kaffirs' she must rub herself all over with red ochre to give warning to men of her temporarily changed status.[16]

In highland Papua New Guinea[17] menstruating woman could be made to spend up to four to five years in a palm leaf cage upon coming of age where she was forbidden to touch the ground. In British Columbia the woman was painted red every day and had to wear a conical hat to mark her out, much like a witch's hat, and prevent her from being touched by the sun.[18] In Nigeria[19] there are nomad peoples who will not even allow men and women to touch when women are bleeding.

These accounts could actually go on and on honestly, drawing from many different cultures around the world. The point here is not just to illustrate the intensity of these beliefs, otherwise I might have gone into more detail about the scenarios where the menstruating woman is buried up to her neck in hot sand for days, but will instead focus on specific reoccurring mythic tremors. One of the things that keeps coming up over a widespread area is a taboo against bleeding on the ground, being sewn into a hammock, or suspended in a cage so as not

28

to touch the ground, not looking at men with the blasting gaze, touching food, drinking from springs or teats, or seeing the sun.

It is fair to say that in a great many cultures around the world, of which European countries[20] cannot be said to be exempt, a menstruating woman changed status in her society during the bleed, and not usually in a way that could be said to be for the better. For this reason bleeding women can be said to occupy a strange liminal relationship to the rest of their community, in that they were, and are, temporary and cyclic bearers of witch-blood, even if they don't practice witchcraft. This fact does not seem to me to be irrelevant when meditating on women's strong but non-exclusive traditional association with sorcery. Matthew Hopkins, the famous hunter of witches outrightly made the connection.[21] He put it that Satan would use the fallen 'organs of that body to speak withal to make his compact up with the witches.' Whilst men are involved in witchcraft too, they seem to be characterised as catching it from women, whether physically embodied women, such as their mothers or wives, or ancestor women who open gateways to the sky. The witch-blood and the menstruous blood seem to be inherently mythically co-mingled.

Now that we have looked at the menstruating woman as a temporary Person of the Outside and this example of supposed ritual uncleanliness, let's look specifically at the taboo against touching the earth that is mentioned by Frazer in *The Golden Bough* which he covers in Chapter 1: 'Not to Touch the Earth'. This focus on special tracks that the bleeding woman must try to traverse, avoiding crossing over with tracks used only by men and non-bleeding people, is probably the most geographically far-reaching rule, from some Aboriginal Australian peoples, to similar restrictions found in Africa, two places where the populations have been separated for at least ninety-thousand years.

The specific nature of the menstrual taboos, over large distances, and expanses of time suggests it has its source in something ancient, something that very early Sapiens might have originally opposed or Othered. This taboo is also made extra impactful by common rites involving preventing the bleeding woman from touching the earth at all during her menstruation, in this way she is not allowed to make herself more powerful over the group, she is not allowed to ground the uncanny force seen as moving through her into the same sacred tracks as others use. What can we understand from this reaction to a natural and necessary bodily function?

To try to scry into this phantom story lurking underneath the surface of the bloodied waters of menstruation let us invoke also the ghosts of another group of people who in the past were marked as unclean, and who were tabooed in various ways that are similar to those imposed upon menstruating women. The Cagots — a minority group found in Spain, France, and Basque territories — who are attested to as early as the 1300's but likely existed beforehand are described thus:

> *In appearance they were fair and physically underdeveloped and had narrow, pointed heads. De Rochas states that they had, by way of hair, a kind of very blond down and that their shrivelled nails curled over the quick at the end of their fingers. Their ears lacked a lower lobe and, if one is to believe popular tradition unequal in size, with one being covered in hair.*[22]

There are many theories about the Cagot's unclean social status, from them being seen as the descendants of leper colonies, through to being a racial minority of some other mysterious, and mythically unkind sort. The other popular possibility was that they were descendants of surviving Cathars. This latter claim is worth looking at in terms of the root-system of a legend, even though there is some evidence that Cagots existed before the Cathar persecutions.

After the massacre sometimes referred to as the Albigensian Crusade, the remaining Cathars were obliged by the thirteenth century onward to sew a yellow cross to their clothes to mark them Othered. Notable qualities of the Cathars included a strong focus on Mary Magdalene, and an almost equal spiritual status given to women. They were also accused of sodomy,[23] apparently as a means to avoid the evils of reproduction, wishing as they did to avoid creating more corporeal suffering. All of this dehumanisation of Cathars (required psychologically for the unthinkable cruelties inflicted upon them) touched on deep concerns of what the church would deem 'the feminine'.

Even if Cagots were connected with another earlier heresy the pattern behind the link seems to be similar and noteworthy. Like the menstruating woman among the Dravidians the Cagot was made to use a separate door, especially in churches. They could not drink from the same water fountain or cup as non Cagots, and were sometimes referred to as ducks, because of the large red duck or goose foot they had to wear to mark themselves out. It was also rumoured that they might actually have webbed feet like a duck or goose.[24]

Cagots were restricted to only three occupations carpenter, butcher, and rope maker. This restriction of trades occurred with the last of these afflicting Cathars as well. Children and grandchildren of condemned Cathars were prohibited from becoming priests, judges, or magistrates, accountants, physicians, surgeons or even shopkeepers.[25] This would have had the effect of keeping their whole bloodline from progressing in society, and of marking that blood-thread out in some way that could not easily disappear, marking those within it as People of the Outside. They could not hold a public office and some penalties could pass from generation to generation without fixed end. Under the statues of limpieza de sangre, the descendants of convicted heretics suffered these disabilities due to 'tainted blood', they were born, and then were forced to endure and die in a state of ritual uncleanliness.

San Benitos[26] worn by heretics were hung up in churches as a badge of shame so everyone could remember which bloodlines had heretics in them. These practices are likely part of the subtle fungal life of ideas that eventually became linked to the concept of witch-blood, the idea of a tainted lineage with an infectious element to it. This dehumanisation of the scapegoat victim on an epic scale embraces centuries of the persecution of heretics. Often it was not heretics or witches who decided they were of the blood but their persecutors. In Europe this ambiguous narrative was co-created between the two groups, and sometimes today the original victim of this story, as with many stories based on violence, reclaims the terms and ideas behind them as a source of personal empowerment.

Whatever the original source of the Cagot bloodline in particular it seems likely that it began with something similar to what happened to the Cathars, who were noted as separate from lepers in the earliest references to them. In this case, with the Cagots believed to bleed from the navel on Good Friday, almost like a form of menstruation, to be possessed of the feet of a duck or goose, and also have differently shaped skulls to other Sapiens we find ourselves in the realm of the only partly human hybrid. There are to be found here in the Cagot history symbols of a different bloodline, of relationships with faerie-lore and secret histories perhaps known only to the insider-outsider. Like many other groups the Cagots were not just symbolically dehumanised, they were being cast as a different species, one that was not allowed to share the same footways with other humans, or walk with bare feet upon the same ground, or drink from the same source. Cagots were also associated with the colour red, much as menstruating women in many cultures were painted red with ochre to identify themselves.

Cagots had to wear a red stitched on goosefoot to be visible to the public, and shake a rattle when they approached, so that nobody was caught in the position of needing to share the road with them. The Cagot was expected to deny their right to gaze upon others with all of their justified resentment, to not look directly at clean people, much like a menstruating woman in many cultures they were not allowed to use her gaze or even handle food for others. The red patch depicting the goose foot was large and visible from a distance on the Cagot's chest, much like the yellow star given to Jews during persecution, or the yellow cross placed on the Cathars.

Tellingly the Cagots were also not allowed to go barefoot lest, again, they pollute the clean pathways. The accusations against the Cagots were a familiar set of stories listed below, claims that no doubt helped people bypass any guilt the exclusion and persecution of the Cagots might have otherwise roused in them.

The claims included: that Cagots were cannibals, practitioners of a sorcery with much in common with witchcraft, heretics, intellectually inferior, cretins, possibly psychotic, sexual deviants, and practitioners of incest (this was likely true as it was enforced by the rules banning Cagots from marrying outside their number with Basque, French, or Spanish people).[27]

Not only did they possess navels that wept blood on Good Friday their bodies gave off an unusual amount of heat. When the south wind blew their lips, jugulars, and a duck-foot mark under their left arm all swelled up.[28] Apparently they also had a strange smell. Here we see a number of characteristics that associate them with witches, especially the artificial or perhaps inborn(?) mark of an animal's foot under the left armpit. You might say quite simply that, like many minorities, they were feared because they were persecuted, (and therefore might be imagined to seek revenge), and they were persecuted because they were feared.[29] The goose or duck foot is crucial to understanding the flavour of this Othering, because both are mentioned as forms the devil might take in Gregory IX 1233 Vox in Rama where the devil is described as appearing as a toad, but sometimes a goose or duck.[30]

Throughout European folklore having one webbed duck or goose foot connects you with powerful female figures, such as Dame Holda, Berchta, La Reine Pedauque, even the Queen of Sheba, and (importantly given the prevalence of the Cagot in Basque territory) the Basque lamia (faerie creature). When a lamia, goddess, or sorcerer queen has this feature it is usually covered up by her skirt not blazoned on her chest, seen as a hidden imperfection to her beauty or a strangeness of gait, one that she is often trying to hide and embarrassed to have revealed. Unlike Sapiens she finds it harder to conceal her connection with animality.

This symbol the Cagots were forced to wear which echoed the hidden mark under their left arm has pagan and faerie-lore roots, but it's also one with distinctly feminine connotations. Mother Goose imagery is only associated with women after all, and no male lamia I've come across is described with the webbed feet that the Cagot also shared, though, due to the contagion of being Otherwise, the Cagot men as well as women possess this trait. Being a goose was a slang term for a prostitute in the past, and is also used to this day in Britain for behaving like a fool, so it's fair to say that association with this animal was not necessarily always meant respectfully.

What it meant to the Cagots themselves to have this enormous symbol stitched onto their clothing, reminding the public of their alleged hidden mark, and all these other constant reminders of being unclean, we can only imagine. Sadly we know that sharing water fountains and wearing badges were forms of exclusion that continued up until disgracefully recently under segregation in America, and during Nazi persecution of Jewish people. Just as we are forced to imagine the psychological impact on bleeding women the world over, where their cultures believed their blood polluted the track or water-way so strongly it could do men to death, we are forced to imagine them kept away from the sun, their fellows, excluded from sacred doings, and sometimes under-nourished, and even being hoodwinked.

When one tries to imagine living in the place of the witch-bloodied figure, and the impact it must have had on the person who may or may not have had any say in it, it is difficult to find a reason to defend such practices. It is important to remember that Christian religion[31] in the past disallowed certain things during menstruation too, and believed that a woman was unclean and capable of infecting others with a taint, one that also remained on her for longer after childbirth if she gave birth to a girl child, than a boy. So, feelings of cultural superiority are unwarranted by any member of Sapiens when it comes to this species of cruelty, or of inflicting undignified experiences on disempowered groups.

The notion of hair upon the Cagot's single strange ear should also be discussed, for its asymmetry, providing a suggestion of being half one thing, half another, but also for the hair itself and with its animal connotations. It appears the Cagot is unclean through association with things often attributed to women, faeries, and animals. Anyone with a knowledge of the extensive history of misogyny which goes far beyond what is discussed above would have to find the combination of accusations of being: intellectually inferior, crazy, witchcraft practicing, a goose or duck foot possessing person who is forbidden to touch the ground lest they sully it, to be strongly redolent of symbols used against women. As incest has already been spoken-for one must also suspect that the type of sexual deviancy levelled at the Cagot, like the Cathars, might be sodomy, and with it the assumption of non-reproductive sex, and for men the connotation of unmanliness, that it often carries in societies with a thorough hatred for receptive bodies.

The asymmetrical nature of the Cagot's ears is reminiscent of the one goose foot of the faerie, or one goat's foot of the devil, and various goddesses. In this case the uncanny aspect is likely to be due to the belief in the Cagot's degeneracy, but, of course, the suggestion they were also somehow more animal than everyone else. Hair has a strange relationship with magic, the unclean, and the holy all at once. It's fair to say there is something lurking under the water line of the human psyche when it comes to our relationship with our animal self. Something that's been bothering us far earlier than when Darwin wrote *The Origin of the Species*.

It is a something we are at once at pains to repress, to prevent it leaking out of us, getting in the water like a blood rush, seeping into the sacred trackways, or seeping up into a man who tries to rest on the bed where that magic occurred. To exclude it, to avoid contamination with it, to exile it both from ourself and our communities, and at the same time we remain, as a species, fascinated and in some cases repulsed by this power.

Like the ear of the Cagot, we find hairiness in a number of places. May Moulach, a well-known Scottish brownie who performed household tasks, also helped the head of the Grant family defeat opponents at chess, and behaved as a banshee to the family announcing upcoming deaths. She too was in possession of a magical asymmetry, being a hairy left hand and arm.[32] This is not the only example of hair covered beings as a gateway to magic, and, of course, the left hand is the witch's hand where a Witch Mark is often drawn.

In medieval Britain we also find this association between being hirsute and wise. Gerald of Wales recorded a tale of a hairy woman spirit who acts as an initiator of occult skills:

In our time a Welshman named Melerius, who,... having on a certain night...met a damsel whom he had long loved. While he was indulging in her embraces, suddenly, instead of a beautiful girl, he found in his arms a hairy, rough, and hideous creature.[33]

The man was apparently deprived of his senses simply by seeing her body hair! He was only put back into a sane state of mind by the saints. Gerald admits though that via his:

extraordinary familiarity with unclean spirits, by seeing them, talking with them, and calling each by his proper name, he was enabled, through their assistance to foretell future events.

Here we see that the spirit is designated unclean through being hair-covered but also possesses the ability to tell the future. Much like the Witch of Endor, who outperformed God.

The figure of the wild-man or woman is ubiquitous in the folklore of many nations, from the beginning of recorded literature where Enkidu, the wild-living, blood-brother of Gilgamesh, through to wild-woman figures like the Basa Anderea, being hair covered can also be associated with wisdom, virtue, and even asceticism. This ambiguity, where unclean spirits give people power over divination means extra hair is a signal that can mean either unclean or very virtuous makes hairiness a truly liminal characteristic. Enkidu, like the Basa Juan, (Basa Anderea's wild man husband) not only is hairy all over and agile as a deer but protects herds and flocks. With the sexual and grooming administrations of Shamhat, a holy whore figure, he becomes civilised only after his body hair is cut and groomed by her. When he enters the world of man he proves intelligent, though perhaps in some ways lacking in refinements! Considering *The Epic of Gilgamesh* is almost four thousand years old it has been discussed whether this blood brotherhood between Gilgamesh and his savage companion Enkidu represents a long term folk memory of the fundamental connection between Sapiens and the Elder Folk usually known scientifically as the Neanderthals?

Even at an unconscious level the way Enkidu is put forward as a kind of spiritual twin of Gilgamesh's, without which he is incomplete and quite frankly rather violently insane, is very suggestive. If taken this way it could be said that this story mythologises the flaws of Sapiens very adroitly. The same question has been asked about the Basa Juan — a form of wild man believed to live in the forests and mountains of the Basque province. Until recently the idea of a folk memory of Europe's original inhabitants sounded unlikely, partially because the Basa Juan was said to have taught the ancestors of the Basques a great number of skills, including that of metal working which was never part of the toolkit of the Elder Folk.

These days though we know that whilst the Elder Folk in Europe weren't forging metal, when the ancestors of modern man entered that land the Neanderthals may indeed have already been doing art earlier than our Sapien ancestors.[34] At the very least we can be assured their knowledge of the land and capability with dealing with the cold were far beyond our ancestor's abilities. Or given that most of us have 1-3% of our DNA made up of Neanderthal genes perhaps we is just as appropriate as us? Of course, this very topic, this matter of who is an us and who is a them is very much at the heart of our meditations on scapegoats and outsider blood.

Given that Tasmanian Aboriginal people preserved stories that seem to remember the icebergs in the sea during the last Glacial Maximus we know that it is not impossible that oral memory, dream-scaped into enduring mythos, can survive for tens of thousands of years. We also know that artificial cranial deformation, a practice of binding a baby's soft head into a shape that helps to elongate the back of the skull to appear more like the shape of a Neanderthal skull appears all over the world in seemingly disconnected locations. Places as far flung as the Kimberley in Australia and Toulouse in France seem to have independently come up with the idea that it made people wiser, higher born, or more spiritual, to bind in this manner.

I mention this binding practice because part of the physical difference attested for the Cagot is a narrow, pointed back of the head. Whilst it might not seem immediately Neanderthal-connected it is interesting that the Shandar skeletons of the Elder Folk were originally believed to be so unusually distinct as to be artificially cranially deformed. We now know that's likely just what their heads looked like.[35] It is surely worth noticing that the pre-colonial standards of beauty among head-binding people in the Philippines, for instance, involved flattening the forehead, extending the back of the head and widening the face till both were of roughly the same length and width.[36] This is fascinating in how, much like the image of the Toulouse deformity in France, the use of which reached right up to the twentieth century eliminated some of the most obviously Sapien features of the skull. Not to mention the more negatively framed pointed heads of the Cagots. Whilst in broadly Asian and South American cultures this shape is generally associated with the nobility, in Toulouse it was considered to be the behaviour of peasants.

Areas where head binding or occipital accentuation endured for longer may have resulted from an attempt to shape our own skulls to look more like those of early hybrid people. We need only remember that the Philippines and other Asiatic areas practicing head binding would more likely to have been copying the head shape of Denisovans than drawing entirely from Neanderthals.[37] The way that we treat body hair and wild people figures in stories is also highly suggestive that what is in one context deemed unclean, is in another seen as holy.

In fact, as a species we are altogether mixed up about what we feel towards these hybrid elements in our own nature. Wild women like Mis in Irish culture go mad with grief and end up becoming covered, much like Sapsorrow in the fairytale, with fur and feathers. The gentle harpist, Dubh Ruis, coaxed her into a pool and gently washed away the fur and feathers and makes love to her, reclaiming her from the wild much as Shamhat did for Enkidu, through sex, kindness, and personal grooming. Mis also links this wild woman trope with blood drinking, a form of cannibalism, as her madness is made clear by her extreme grief causing her to drink of her fallen father's blood.[36]

The status of these wild women reclaimed, like Mis and Sapsorrow — also known as Straggle-tag — is redeemed, but still ambiguous, perhaps some taint of the wild remains under the surface of her bare skin. The hair-covered figure who is more explicitly allowed to be holy is Mary Magdalene, after her hermitage in a French mountain cave, she is depicted as having been in the wilderness so long her clothing had simply fallen apart. Much like Mis who has a cat-like soft fur all over her, the Magdalene was said to have grown body hair all over in such a way that it shielded her modesty.

She was covered by hair this way during her ascension to Heaven. Given the area of France where the Magdalene underwent this transformation into a holy wild woman being so close to Basa Anderea territory, the Toulouse cranial deformity, some of the later holdout sites of the Neanderthals, the Cagot and Cathar persecutions, and a major witchcraft hotspot, it is certainly a tap-root of power to see this all over body hair associated with a saint... Somewhere at the centre of all these taboos is a nexus, or even a nimbus, of holy-hood.

Notes

1. Alison Hanham, The Scottish Hecate: a wild witch chase Scottish Studies. 13: 59–64.

2. A most notable example of this is how Isabel of Spain gave the command that conquistadors were only allow to enslave a population if they were proven cannibals. The result of this is that a lot of populations were declared to be

cannibals. This, of course, does not mean that cannibalism didn't exist only that the reports of colonisers regarding people eating must be ingested with a pinch of salt.

3. Mircea Eliade, *Birth and Rebirth: the Religious Meaning of Initiation in Human Cultures*, Harper and Brothers, New York, 1958, Chapters II and III.

4. Gooch, Ibid., p.1820.

5. H. G. Wolf, 'Cultural Conceptualizations of Magical Practices Related to Menstrual Blood in a Transhistorical and Transcontinental Perspective'. Cultural-Linguistic Explorations into Spirituality, Emotionality, and Society, (2021) chapter: 14, p. 47.

6. Walter O. Weyrauch, *Gypsy Law: Romani Legal Traditions and Culture*, University of California Press, 13 Aug 2001p.157.

7. James George Frazer. *The Golden Bough: A Study in Magic and Realism*, a New Abridgement from the Second and Third Editions. New York: Oxford UP, 1994, ch.8.

8. Rita E. Montgomery, 'A Cross-Cultural Study of Menstruation, Menstrual Taboos, and Related Social Variables', Ethos Vol. 2, No. 2 (Summer, 1974) pp.140-141.

9. Frazer, op cit., ch.8.

10. Ruth Benedict, *Patterns of Culture.*, Houghton Mifflin, 2005. The Talmud – Seder Tohoroth (The Book of Cleanliness) spends 509 pages describing how one can know whether someone is clean or not based on discharge colouration.

11. trans J. Darmesteter, The Zend-avesta, Oxford, (1880).

12. Frazer, op cit., ch.8.

13. Jacqueline H. Harris, (2022). George MacDonald's 'Frightening Female: Menopause and Makemnoit in The Light Princess'., p.26, 12 November 2022, from https://digitalcommons.snc.edu/cgi/viewcontent.cgi?article=1205&context=northwind

14. Frazer, op cit., ch.8.

15. Y. Mohamed, K. Durrant, C. Hugget, J. Davis, A. Macintyre, & S. Menu, et al. (2018). A qualitative exploration of menstruation-related restrictive practices in Fiji, Solomon Islands and Papua New Guinea. PLOS ONE, 13(12), p.1, e0208224. doi: 10.1371/journal.pone.0208224.

16. Frazer, op cit., p.703.

17. Mette Bovin, *Nomads Who Cultivate Beauty: Wodaabe Dances and Visual Arts in Niger.*, The Nordic Africa Institute (2001) p.11.

18. Rita A. Montgomery, p.139.

19. Madeleine F. Ott, 'Impure Blood: The Menstrual Taboo in the Christian Church During the Thirteenth Century', St. Mary's Academy2021). Retrieved 25 December 2021, from https://pdxscholar.library.pdx.edu/cgi/viewcontent.cgi?article=1143&context=younghistorians

20. *Matthew Hopkins, The Discovery of Witches: In Answer to Several Queries, Witches of the Atlantic World: A Historical Reader and Primary Sourcebook.* Ed. Elaine G. Breslaw. New York, (2000). 37-41.

21. Rodney Gallop, *A Book of the Basques.*, Macmillan, London1970. p.58.

22. Stephen O'Shea, *The Perfect Heresy: The Revolutionary Life and Death of the Medieval Cathars.*, New York: Walker & Company, (2000) pp.80-81.

23. Cabarrouy, Jean-Emile 'The Cagots, Excluded and cursed from the southern lands'. J. & D. éditions. (1995).

24. John Guy, Humiliation: A Theme in Ecclesiastical Folklore, (2022). p.78. Retrieved 13 November 2022, from https://www.proquest.com/openview/271bf49582fc2e99eccf9d13e1d76761/1?pq-origsite=gscholar&cbl=2026366&diss=y

25. Guy, Ibid., p.68.

26. Rodney Gallop, *The Book of the Basques.*, University of Nevada Press, (1970) pp.58-59.

27. Daniel Hawkins, 'Chimeras that degrade humanity: the cagots and discrimination'., Academia Paper, (2014) p.7.

28. Robb, Graham (2007). *The Discovery of France: a historical geography from the Revolution to the First World War*. New York London: W.W. Norton & Company.

29. Cohn, op cit., p.49.

30. 'If you touch any object she has sat on, you must wash your clothes and bathe yourself in water, and you will remain unclean until evening. This includes her bed or any other object she has sat on; you will be unclean until evening if you touch it. If a man has sexual intercourse with her and her blood touches him, her menstrual impurity will be transmitted to him.' (Lev. 15:22-24).

31. Sir Walter Scott, 'Minstrelsy of the Scottish Border Consisting of Historical. and Romantic Ballads, collected in southern counties of Scotland; with a few of modern date founded upon local tradition.' Project Gutenberg eBook. (2021). cxiv 24 December 2021, from https://www.gutenberg.org/files/12742/12742-h/12742-h.htm

32. Gerald of Wales, *Vision of Britain*, Book I, Ch. 5: Usk and Caerleon. (2021). Retrieved 25 December 2021, from https://www.visionofbritain.org.uk/traveller

33. D. L. Hoffmann, et al, The dating of carbonate crusts reveals Neandertal origin of Iberian Cave Art. Science, 359, 6378.

34. Francis Ivanhoe, Erik Trinkaus, On Cranial Deformation in Shanidar 1 and 5 | Current Anthropology: Vol 24, No 1. (2022). Current Anthropology. Retrieved from https://www.journals.uchicago.edu/doi/abs/10.1086/202956?journalCode=ca

35. Scott, William Henry (1994). *Barangay: Sixteenth-century Philippine Culture and Society*. Ateneo University Press. p. 22.

36. Preliminary estimates based on Denisovan genetic clues suggest that they had a flattened forehead, flat top of the head, extended back of the skull, matched by the widest face among any other homo species previously known.

37 Danielle Marie Cudmore, agus ag ól a fola: Ingesting Blood and Engendering Lament in Medieval Irish Literature. (2021) Brill, pp.165-189. Retrieved from https://brill.com/display/book/9789004499690/BP000019.xml

Chapter 4

Cannibal of the Outside

One of the prime accusations made against Cagots, witches, and even the Templars is that of cannibalism. Andrew McGowan in his paper 'Eating People' discusses the way cannibalism was used in the past (and maybe still is) to make the ultimate claim of inhumanity against a person or people. A vastly more sophisticated swerve than the refusal of eye-contact Sugito used when he murdered Doe, but nonetheless a reflex that serves the same purpose of denying personhood to another group.

Ultimately the Roman state was about to murder a great deal of Christians instead of an Orangutang, and to better do so they needed to be classified as what was called a 'third race', or a 'dog-eyed' people[1] who were so uncivilised that they actually consumed human flesh, and were therefore a risk to the whole Roman way of life. It is interesting as an aside that they were right about the threat Christianity played to the Roman pagan way of life, as can be appreciated by an understanding of later history. If one's Roman pagan aim was to reinforce continuity, then the fear they felt of Christians was evidently quite justified, as this new sect would go on to eventually replace their whole way of life.

The Greek philosophers who underpinned Roman thinking alluded to the belief that animal sacrifice was at some level a replacement for previous rituals of human sacrifice. Some philosophers like Pythagoras and Empedocles went as far as to suggest that to eat animals, being they are our brothers and sisters, was also a form of cannibalism. Somewhere lurking under the surface of the group psyche was this idea that in their own less civilised past there was a time of cannibalism for which we were still substituting animals.

Perhaps in some epigenetic way[2] this was a particularly strong haunting, this memory, as it came up again during the revolting persecution of the Cathars and Templars. The details of the work of the Spanish Inquisition against these sects remains among the most intense human rights violations I have encountered. I think this very human point is an important one to make when we think about the ways these cruelties were storied into being, because these were terrible mistakes made around our sense of belonging and non-belonging, insider and outsider, around our need for homogeneity, and our fear of change. These mistakes were caused by failures in our rituals, failures with appropriately managing our own savagery, threat response, and emotional inclusion needs.

Somewhere along the thousand years in between this persecution an arm of Christianity later began to then beat unto others what had previously been beaten into them. Sometimes worse things were done on a larger scale, and to also accuse others of precisely what they were once accused of... It behooves us as People of the Outside to try to understand how this process happened, to get better at intellectually stepping outside of our allegiances, and hopefully in this understanding learn better methods for avoiding any future repetitions. Whether or not we will even have the power to prevent such things is moot, what matters more is that somehow, somewhere someone has done this imaginative work at comprehending what happens psychologically before a pogrom starts.

How can we manage our sense of belonging and our need for sameness more skilfully? Less brutally? If Sapiens cannot outrightly avoid savagery how can we do better at sublimating it into ritual forms where the outcome is more controlled and regulated? What is the use of history at all if we cannot utilise it to cry out against repetitions of this sort of outrage? Nobody ever knows if they belong to a group that could be targeted, given that being Christian has not saved people in the past.

So, we return to the point the mill of this book turns around in meditative slowness: how do we meet the ghost of the cannibal? Who originally begot these unclean bloodlines of heretics, discriminated against for centuries after the crime? And how through this history might we better come to understand the concept of witch-blood? Who is this shadow race within a race that everyone from Roman pagans, to medieval Christians were so afraid of, and did not wish to be like so much they denied humanity to them and killed people in despicable ways? Who is the phantasmagoria they strived to exorcise from their communities, and themselves?

Luckily we stand at a privileged moment in history where advances in dating samples and genetics allows us access to information that makes us better able to answer some of these questions. Not only do People of the Outside get access to both a voice with which to talk back and access to a gaze, but we can put those hands and eyes to what might amount to some of the closest to unbiased sources of information Sapiens has ever had access to. It doesn't mean that all things called science are free of human bias, this is unlikely as the material is generated and then interpreted by humans, but we do find that sometimes we know things that do not support our view of ourselves, and are therefore far more likely to be real.

Here's something we know about ourselves — our ancestors were cannibals. We inherit a resistance to prion disease[3] which is primarily passed down to us through generations of the eating of the human brain. The fact that some of our ancestors, including pre-Sapien ancestors developed this resistance after considerable exposure tells us that there was a lot of human brains consumed for a sustained period of time to allow this quality to develop.

The earliest evidence of the remains left by a cannibal meal can be attributed to pre-Neanderthal ancestors various called Heidelbergensis. As they were likely the root source of both

Neanderthals in the west, and Denisovans in the east, some people have been playfully calling them 'Neandersovans'. In their cave they very clearly had a big meal of people over 150,000 years ago.[4] The bones don't appear to have been treated as special, but were disposed of along with the bones of other food animals — unless, of course, all the animal bones were special in some way there is no way to delineate the hominid members.

During what looks like a tough time of population bottleneck in Europe we also find a later Neanderthal cave home with a whole family of other Neanderthals whose bones were smashed for marrow extraction, and all the usual signs of de-fleshing and brain eating. These human bones were also disposed of on the bone pile, the same place where the bones of the other eaten animals went after dinner. Whether this was indicative of ritual is a question we might still ask, but if it was then it's likely so was the consumption of other animals.[5]

Before we allow this to make us feel superior to our cousins, and also forebears, we should note that there are also sites that suggest our own Sapien ancestors eating Neanderthals, and our ancestors eating each other, and making each other's skulls into drinking vessels and other tools around 15,000 years ago.[6] Of course, we can't infer much about context from these remains. We can also imagine that predation cannibalism might have been involved in the whole family feast in the late Neanderthal period. What we can't know is whether it was casual and predation cannibalism which was regularly repeated? Or was it scarcity induced killing? Or expedient cannibalism during a crisis where the death has already occurred? Or ritual mortuary cannibalism of loved ones? Was the entire bone heap sacred and disposal not as disrespectful as it appears? Or was cannibalism even a shameful example of a crime in their culture?

Given that all of these behaviours have also happened among different Sapien cultures, at one time, place, or another, it doesn't seem too much of a stretch to suggest that other hominid species had similar levels of variation. It is often easy to forget the variety of behaviour currently seen around the globe in our not particularly genetically diverse species. I say all this because cannibalism has been used very effectively as a motif to Otherwise people, that we forget there are numerous ways and cultural motifs under which it can occur.

Cannibalism and the lack of it, as part of the scaffolding for the construction of the idea of a human being, and the all-too necessary partner, the inhuman, has still been very much in use in in recent history as well. Part of the image-violence that has been wrought upon numerous indigenous people by colonialism has involved the charge of cannibalism. To the extent that Spanish slave taking was not allowed by decree of Queen Isabel unless that people were guilty of cannibalism.[7]

Naturally, the conquistadors found a great many cannibals in the parts of the world they visited... This is not to say that cannibalism was not practiced, but under the influence of colonialism the context and actual extent is obscured. When you consider the frequent cannibalism that seems to have happened among our fellow hominid species it could make sense as a test for who is human, all except for those caves in Somerset where our own ancestors were eating people and making things from their bones, and, of course, a variety of parts of the world where it was or is practiced including the Papua New Guinean highlands,[8] and, of course, the odd plane crash and shipwrecked party.

The use of the Somerset skull caps seems to suggest a form of ritual which shows a sophisticated culture of cannibalism, with the beginning of a sublimation process of mankind's seeming fairly frequent desire to eat each other. Starting with skull kitchenware and bone ritual items we get to look in on the start of a process via which cannibalism becomes more and more symbolic, less actual, until eventually animals will replace humans, and later still red wine will symbolise blood. During any good sublimation event the energy must be transformed successfully without being squashed, this is part of what ritual can do for Sapiens. The memory of the original drive persists and migrates into mythic form, a transformation magic possessed by stories acted out by adults.

The man-eating ogre of fairytales, the inhuman monster-witch consuming children in the woods, the troll, the vampire or wolf-turning one who feeds on human flesh, often feeds upon the innocent flesh of children. The appearance of the ogre or flesh eating wild man is big and hairy, and the witch stereotype sports a heavy brow ridge, a protruding hooked nose, and large teeth, much like the Elder Folk. Upon her head sits the cone shaped hat, emphasising the back of her head and making it appear larger than it is, similar to the pointy hat of the menstruating woman, to those placed on victims by the inquisition, and even the more recently the dunce-cap.

The pointier back of the head of the Cagots was despised, and yet in other parts of the world there was also the artificial cranial deformation practices, where some cultures have also actively tried to look like the apparently despised and repressed parts of who we are... Science, of course, has also allowed us to know this truth about ourselves in certain ways we couldn't have even one hundred years ago. That no matter how unclean, how taboo, how counter-moving to the general rhythm of the majority of ourselves it may be, at least one, to three types of hominids bred with our Sapien ancestors. By one way of looking at it, the inhuman is truly lurking among us with unknown intentions towards the surviving society, but also inside us, just as the most fervent of our persecutors always feared.

In our early example of unclean conspirators, the deviant sect known as early Christians, we find that the element of blood drinking is as important as the flesh-eating — as the eucharist attests. There aren't just heretic bloodlines, there are holy ones where blood drinking or sharing links people together, as happens in the practice of blood-brotherhood, or in the previously mentioned belief that the Irish drank the blood of their dead. In fact, the idea that some kind of power was gained by virtue of these early heretics drinking blood together comes up in the lurid writings about their supposed ways. The ritual cleanliness status of blood in general, and menstrual blood in particular, are key anxieties that large numbers of Sapien cultures seem to share.

All of this makes us think that the consuming of red flesh, red blood, stigmatised ochre red-painted girls, scarlet women, red-handed faeries, red goose feet sewn onto clothes, and the Red Lord of the Basque witches, are all a part of the traces of a ghost species. Like the two different looking ears of the Cagot, there is a memory of something old beyond measure, something that catches the past red-handed, red as the earliest ochre handprints. Something that would have been long forgotten, even subconsciously forgotten, if we were not all of our ancestors walking.

Out of all the ritualised scapegoats, witches alone hold the distinction of being an alembic for the processing of every form of sublimated cannibalism. By the time the witchcraft trials took up the persecution baton from the Templars and the Bogomils, witches were connected with a variety of forms of taking. They didn't just poison wells like lepers and Jews were supposed to do, they skimmed the cream off the milk, the fat off the land, the sheen off the crops, the baby from the womb, the vigour from the man's member, they blighted with their gaze or with a fated dart that picked off those who were doomed to die.

Even when witches appeared to give to their community through healing it was believed to be only possible by blighting someone elsewhere with the same ill they had removed, even if this was as simple as the toad magic in West Country England, where the sickness was given to the animal. For anyone who understands how nature works knows that there is no boon in one place that does not take a little cream from some other place. Due to a difficult and dangerous life many of our early-modern ancestors were likely far less sentimental about the harsh facts of life than many of us are today. For them witches ate people, often literally, but always metaphorically, symbolically, magically, for what is a slow social death but a death by a thousand paper cuts from sharp tongues and ill-wishing onlookers?

Witches had been of concern to Apuleius some fifteen hundred years earlier and their sorcery forbidden hundreds of years earlier still, long before Christ. Yet in the early modern period they became a fully blown conspiracy, one of a long history of such state religion, or empire-wide, hysterias. Of course, there was a very well-developed social counter-narrative going back to the first century to work with so the entire disaster did not need to make itself. There were already heretic descendant populations with hundreds of years' worth of ancestral burden being made pariahs over generations, and no doubt, though their voices have been effectively silenced, their gaze blooded over with a blackthorn attack above the breath, their ghosts were still watching.

Over time they had surely been growing their own response-stories and mythos of themselves and how their situation came to be. These counter-stories likely became our notions of witch-blood. Though they have not been recorded, as the voices of the People of the Outside seldom have been, we can imagine them talking to their children about how their 'tainted blood' was actually something special, something with an extra bit of fire in it, that the bulk of people just didn't understand. No doubt they made their forebears who may have died at the hands of the authorities into martyrs, just as the early Christian did.

By the time witches became the most hated and feared group there were no doubt already numerous networks of sanctioned populations and bloodlines deemed heretical that might easily have identified with the figure of the witch. Given that some of the earlier depictions of witches flying on brooms are actually Waldensian heretic women and that the same charges had been made against them as against witches show us there is a mycelium network linking these persecutions together. Everybody gets the devil they deserve, you might say, and if ancestral witch-bloodlines did not already exist before the hunting of witches became de jour then it would not seem unlikely it would have come to afterwards.

A population when vilified and demeaned for long enough is likely to create a counter-narrative that upholds themselves as misunderstood saviours, merely for psychological self-preservation. As we have said above they fear the Cagot because the Cagot was persecuted and may fight back, they persecuted the Cagot because they were afraid he would fight back. But the Cagot and the Waldensian stories are lost, we do not hear from them as individuals, about how they saw their place in the world at both a cosmic and social level, unlike witches today, they did not get to tender their counter-story to the public, defend themselves, or share their word-spells with us.

For much the same reason witchcraft may have been suspected of women primarily because women were the ones who were being controlled and repressed, therefore there is a fear they will rebel. It appears somewhat heartening when you consider that even violent patriarchs feel enough about what they are doing to other humans who happen to be women that they must create terrifying images of women's magic. There is a sense that somehow women were more connected to the feral, moon-aligned, animal-riding part of our hybrid psyche, the parts those religions sought to oppress.

Of course, the whole of society agreed to rail against the Cagot, the Cathar, the Waldensian, and their men as well as their women. So it is usually true to say that no one oppresses another human without also oppressing themselves through the very consciousness of that unhappiness, anger, and potential vengeful magic of the one oppressed. Given all the angst that arises you would almost think we were just better off not engaging in inhumane forms of oppression of others at all...

The other very common form of cannibalism that witches, early-Christians, and various heretics were accused of was eating babies, and in the case of witches using their fat for ointments. The connection with ointments is intriguing, as if one believes in the sorcerous power of baptism to place the church inside the body of a person one would likely also say that an unbaptised baby would have the purest sort of unclaimed fat in their body. Though, of course, it also acts as a great incentive to have your children baptised if it is rumoured to protect them from witches. As the Christians were also accused of eating babies we can safely say this accusation has more to it than a simple statement of reality.

Baby eating is a potent form of cannibalism to level against someone or some other group because it takes a knock at the foundations of humanity. The fat stealing of unbaptised babes and the taking of pieces of corpses has a chance of having a basis in fact, however, because the suspicion is a little older.[9] There was also a popular tradition of trying to, or actually burning, children suspected of being a changeling so as to frighten the Good Folk out of them, or simply to dispose of them. If this was practiced by non-witches one can't say for sure that already dead babies have not been ransacked for parts by actual witches, or thrown into ovens by ordinary folk on the suspicion of being elf-get.

By and large though it seems likely that the idea of witches in particular cooking babies, such as in Hansel and Gretel and Baba Yaga, could be a misunderstanding of a Slavic custom that survived in Russia, Siberia, the Baltic and the Ukraine, whereby a child that failed to thrive was rebaked. This procedure called perepekaniye, zapekaniye, or dopekaniye.[10] A witch would take the child and place it into damp dough in a warm but not hot oven and as the dough proofed and rose the child was instructed to rise with it.

What is interesting about this harmless process is that there was a granny healer or avowed witch present at the time and it was her job to take away the contaminated rye dough at the end of the ritual. Sometimes she would take it with the child still inside it and the mother would wail and weep at the loss of her child to this symbolic death. After which the child would be restored to her afresh as a new child. Here it was the witch's job to discard the unwanted dough and the residue of that other sick child that had been baked away. It seems possible that such rituals were part of the way witches came to be associated with cooking and feasting on babies, as the witch was indeed involved in 'feasting' on the residue when it was discarded, an instance where pseudo-cannibalism can be done as an act of healing.

Cannibalism is sometimes more subtle than the actual eating of human flesh. It might involve drawing off life essence from people or their crops, sometimes that life essence is diseased, sometime it's healthful. Witches are known to have this ability inherently, whether as a skill or affliction, it has a lot to do with their connection with the realm of the dead. It is also something that many groups of Sapiens have probably ascribed to people they suspected of thriving during tough times, but potentially true in some cases. Skimming the cream off the milk and the vitality from the crops is another form of eating from your neighbour's largesse. Such techniques can be connected to spinning where the fat of the land is taken while the fleece is incorporated turned into thread. The thread then comes to represent the stolen Virtue and can be woven into the clothing of the family.

The aggressive sorcerers (Malandanti) that opposed the Benandanti were trying to steal the seeds and power of the future crops on the behalf of the people of the Underworld. Their allegiance here is complicated. It is possible they weren't connected to living humans as their opposers were, and that the Benandanti were pushed by their inquisitors to connect them with someone that might be tried for the crime. This being said, just because someone is acting against the best interests of the species they belong to does not mean there wasn't someone actually doing this work. Thiess the werewolf, the Benandanti and the Taltos, who all fought night battles in their spirit bodies, all talk about how they got no choice in having the nature they did, and the same may be said for their enemies.[11]

Whilst it might not be quite the same as directly feasting on someone's infant, trying to disadvantage a harvest that your own human body may need to eat certainly results in an outcome that does not advantage your community. As such we might want to look more closely at this, why there would be some people among us that are not as committed, whether they would like to be or not, to the safety and prosperity of other Sapiens. It's almost as though we are, in fact, as a species more than one thing. It's like we have ghosts walking the corridors of our bones, wailing and gnashing their teeth for a chance to express themselves, to further the advantage of the dead.

Notes

1. Andrew McGowan, Eating People: accusations of cannibalism among second century Christians, p.21.

2. A scientific term for what People of the Outside have long been calling ancestral memory.

3. Mark Stoneking, M. (2003). Widespread prehistoric human cannibalism: easier to swallow? Trends In Ecology & Evolution, 18(10), (2003) pp.489-490. Doi: 10.1016/s0169-5347(03)00215-5

4. Eudald Carbonell et al, Cannibalism as a Paleoeconomic System in the European Lower Pleistocene: The Case of Level TD6 of Gran Dolina (Sierra de Atapuerca, Burgos, Spain) | Current Anthropology: Vol 51, No 4. (2022). Current Anthropology. Retrieved from https://www.journals.uchicago.edu/doi/abs/10.1086/653807

5. Elizabeth Culotta, Neanderthals Were Cannibals, Bones Show, Science Vol 286, no.5437, pp.18-19.

6. Silvio Bello, et al, (2015). Upper Palaeolithic ritualistic cannibalism at Gough's Cave (Somerset, UK): The human remains from head to toe. Journal Of Human Evolution, 82, (2015) pp.170-189. Doi: 10.1016/j.jhevol.2015.02.016

7. McKenner Marie Brewer, Jaguars and slaves: European constructions of cannibalism in colonial Latin America – ProQuest. (2022), p.23. Retrieved 13 November 2022, from https://www.proquest.com/openview/fba87f57ee2f14c1eb809839ab44a506/1?pq-origsite=gscholar&cbl=18750

8. Ilka Thiessen, The Social Construction of Gender. Female Cannibalism in Papua New Guinea., Anthropos, Bd.96, H.1 (2001), pp.141-142.

9. I say this simply because stealing parts of corpses for spells is mentioned as early as Apuleius and exists as a parallel as far afield as among Australian sorcerers suggesting a wider coverage for this idea. This is covered in some detail

in A.P Elkin's Aboriginal Men of High Degree which we will attend to again below.

[10] ‎T.A. Listova, A Program for Collection of Material on the Customs and Rituals Associated with Childbirth, Soviet Anthropology and Archeology, (1999) 30:2, pp.53-66, DOI : 10.2753/AAE1061-1959300253.

[11.] Carlos Ginsburg, op cit., ch.3.

Chapter 5

A Night of the Long Teeth

To tease out the elf-locks formed in the hair of a source-story is a delicate business. It seems as though they formed overnight, when no one was watching the horse in its stable, when no gaze fell upon them to interrupt the pixie-braider, and time slips into the sacred still-forming state. We will begin with a few tangles left behind in early Middle Ages Germanic cultures. We have already sifted through the remnants of Roman pagan responses to early Christianity, and the way Christianity and various heresies that followed it were often ascribed some of the same taboo behaviours as witches. An encounter with some early Germanic sources helps us to see similar features from a different watch-post.

In the early Middle Ages, prior to the full Christianisation of the Germanic population there were laws that governed the behaviour and the treatment of the night-witch. By night-witch I mean the involuntary, witch-blooded type who might act as a nightmare. It was illegal in Germany not only to kill a witch but also to eat them afterwards.[1] There is a suggestion inherent here that this practice was common enough that it needed banning. This prohibition against cannibalism was specifically one placed against a folkloric approach to reclaiming stolen power from a Person of the Outside who was viewed as a spiritual aggressor. It is also possible that this reverse cannibalism had something to do with stealing the Virtue of those witches, rather than simply revenge.

Older women in particular were at risk of being eaten because they were believed to gain greater potency over their lifetime. The size of their family was also sometimes seen as indicative of their hidden Virtue, as was the idea that their teeth were able to continue to grow. The longer the teeth became the more powerful the witch.[2] This is, of course, greatly interesting to anyone who is looking for signs that our forgotten and recently re-remembered ancestors with their longer more prominent teeth, sometimes described even in anthropology as 'muzzle like', lie at the source-root of this image bestowed on witches.

One of the most consistent, worldwide, fears we find when it comes to the witching of victims is the theft of a man's sexual potential. It was a matter of some concern in early Germanic sources like *Lex Silica*. A man's virility was to be carefully guarded against the predation of witches. Sorcerers capable of the theft of a man's sex were sometimes men, but the lean in the direction of women is still clear. The taproot of this fear can be revealed by the fact that to deprive a witch of her power required you to lift her clear of the earth,[3] this would be able to break her connection with an unknown source of buried, chthonic power, or to stop her spreading her pollution, and allow for her to be executed. This, of course, links her with menstrual taboos, but also with the Cagot who were not allowed to go barefoot, with their one hairy ear and strangely shaped heads.

Here we are haunted by a spectre that clearly terrified people, one of a woman becoming increasingly powerful as she ages and acquires more grandchildren. This power she has seems to be drawn from the earth and can be grounded back into it, much in the way numerous traditional approaches to menstruation have sought to block it spreading to walking tracks, or even sometimes contact between the blood and the ground itself. Eating the witch who has previously committed some kind of theft is banned, showing us that cannibalism in revenge, as well as in immediate necessity has some kind of mysterious place in the history of European magic.

The long teeth that are thought to grow in size as the witch becomes more powerful place us in mind of non-Sapien species, such as Neanderthals and Denisovans, whose teeth were markedly larger than our own. They also suggest that just as in many fairytales, the witch herself might be the grandmother-bearer of the 'what long teeth you have' story. Like so many before her, whether by a wolf or by a person, she is eaten because she is suspected of eating. To really unravel these tangled locks of mythic hair a little further we will be forced to grapple with the controversial and unusually intense writer, Stan Gooch. Many years before Sapiens were proved to have genetically absorbed Neanderthal ancestors Gooch rightly predicted that modern Sapien was a hybrid between the early-Sapien Cro-Magnon population and Neanderthals. Reality has turned out to be far stranger than fiction in this regard, for whilst he was partially correct he hadn't predicted there were other human species in the mix, such as the Denisovans. Not to mention at least one other extremely archaic ghost population we cannot yet identify with certainty.[4]

It was intuitively correct of Gooch to pick up on our mixed blood and the idea that it creates both advantages in the form of hybrid vigour, and some problems also. Health consequences like autoimmune diseases, and other mental health issues such as seasonal affective disorder are likely connected to our Neanderthal heritage[5] which gave us excellent resistance when moving into new areas, or dealing with ice ages, but came back to bite us with long teeth. Given that the gene for red hair evolved separately among the Elder Folk prior to emerging among Sapiens it might cause us to wonder if the intense reaction to red-heads, usually either distrust (especially of male red-heads who will seldom ever be characterised in movies as anything other than the villain or another untrustworthy sort of man) or fetishistic fascination and attribution of magical abilities.[6] It seems possible that the depth of this feeling might go back further than prejudice against Scottish and Irish people.

There are also a range of weaknesses in Stan Gooch's position that can be attributed to the fact he was born in the 1930's, and didn't seem to remain in touch with changing attitudes around racism. One might say Gooch lost a lot of credibility in holding that the Elder Folk still managed to exist in the wilderness up until the current day. Whilst the literal, manifest yeti angle might sound credulous of him he may have been intuitively correct in another sense. There is currently more of the Elder Folk's DNA living in the world due to population size than there ever has been before despite their 'extinction', so in some sense perhaps he was right. Some of his ideas about who had the most Neanderthal blood were also strongly racially slanted — including the idea that Jewish people had more Neanderthal blood than other cultures based purely on facial feature stereotypes.

Despite these evident flaws in his work what is crucially importantly for us is the connection Gooch made between witchcraft and our Elder Folk ancestors. He picked up on taboos against moving widdershins, left-handedness and left-sidedness, the power of the number thirteen as both unlucky and sacred, and the possible association between the thirteen moons in a year, the value of menstrual or sacrificial blood, highly developed intuitive faculties, and with the Elder Folk's eyes able to better navigate in low light, a preference for night over day. If one considers his work as a whole it contains a well-thought-out case for the idea that similarities in worldwide taboos shared by numerous Sapien cultures throughout the world reflect a memory of an older people. One, I might add, that we likely wouldn't even subconsciously remember at all if not for the fact that both sides live on within us as ancestors.

Gooch postulates that Sapiens at once wanted to banish their religious influence, this includes associating their face shape with brutality and stupidity even though we have no real explanation for why we believe this shape of face belongs to a less intelligent person. Their potential hairiness, especially in Europe, also got a mixed reaction between the hideous and the holy. Sapiens, themselves carry the blood of the Elder Folk, but in the case of Otzi the Iceman, from five thousand years ago, up to ten percent of his genetic material belonged to them.[7]

As a species Sapiens have also been strangely attracted and repelled at the same time — or should we say the different ancestral currents in ourselves have felt these contradictory responses? This conflict, this fear of the inside-outsider, could constitute epigenetic memories of game competition, and perhaps in extreme circumstances predatory cannibalism. Most importantly there is something about all of these witchcraft-associated taboos which is connected with the forbidden. Even today we have Neanderthal Predation Theory (NP) put forward by Danny Vendramini which posits that Neanderthals habitually preyed on Sapiens as food and kidnapped our women for forced sexual encounters. In this theory the face of a Neanderthal is rendered to look like a cross between a hulk-shaped human and gorilla. This 'theory' sounds a lot like the racist, paranoid fears constructed around the fear of African American slaves in America.

Whilst at first glance the wide gulf of time passed between the end of the Elder Folk, or should we say their folding into us, and the gathering of a worldwide belief in malefic witchcraft and humans capable of sending cannibal spirits, this may seem an extreme proposition for Gooch to make but it makes a lot more sense than Vendramini's sensationalist approach to a people who cared for their sick and elderly. Part of the problem with Gooch's work is that it contains this great leap in time. For us, as The People of the Outside, those who acknowledge the ability of ancestors to exist not just in, but as, our very own flesh, to continue to be manifest in us, those who understand that the Older People aren't gone at all might who might be alone in being able to make account for this strange form of genetic haunting.

To alight upon the thorns of reason, so necessary for allowing us to overcome some of the weaker points of emotional impulse, we can see the fundamentally similar Sapien patterns of taboo across wide-ranging geographical locations. We are also left with the idea that humans are able to hang onto emotional logic in the form of mythos for long periods of time. If Sapiens living as far apart as Africa and Australia can share certain almost exact prohibitions around menstruation, then it strikes me that this is likely not to be a matter of oral memory passed down without alteration for over seventy thousand years, but more likely a result of the fact the ancestors continue to be present in our bodies, in new combinations. The past does not disintegrate entirely, it just reweaves again and again and continues to tell its story.

To widen our scope even further for some added perspective the Balinese Layek,[8] a kind of not-all-together human form of witch, to use the English word, engages in what might be termed hag-riding. They have in common with the European witch being a Person of the Outside who is inside but also becomes a nightmare when they sleep. They fly by night and partially consume their prey in cannibalistic predation. They are particularly fond of infants, which might have to do with the idea that rival populations 'steal' infants from each other via birthrates. One of the ways the Layek can be spotted is via their exaggerated sexuality which manifests as a kind of fire, one we may venture to compare to witch-fire, one that seems to focus on their genitals or anus.[9] They also possess the ability to transform into animals.[10]

Witches from Papua New Guinea who are known as ugauga, or men of sorrow, because they are usually widowers, are also known for cannibalising and collecting body substances such as blood and sexual secretions, and for robbing the corpses of the dead.[11] Stephen's paper covers the interesting fact that neither in Bali nor Papua New Guinea did these acts of sorcery and cannibalism originally lead to retaliation. What is crucial about this fact is that it disproves the notion that witchcraft allegations are there solely to provide an opportunity to persecution a particular person or group, though it does not negate the idea that they help the person by attributing blame.

Here in the Papua New Guinean belief, just as in early Germanic laws, can be seen the traditional fear of the sorcerous theft of a man's virility. There is a tight link between fear of witchcraft and a man's fear of loss of his sexual functions. If witchcraft is catching, shared in blood-lines[12] or body fluids, it starts with women's blood, with its history of heavy, worldwide taboos. It seems likely that what we see above the water line is merely the famine stones revealed by the drop in the water we are living through at this moment of historical revelation. These signs are telling us about the silent but impactful presence of a very, very old story indeed.

Stan Gooch was a psychologist by training who went so far as to speak of the legendary and apocryphal sons of god and the daughters of man. He saw them as a mythic structure telling the story of the genetic fusion between Sapien men and women of the Elder Folk, that he insisted occurred as the foundation of our taboos and scapegoating of different groups. If something is ancestrally inside us then it is a bit hard to leave it behind simply because there are no longer any immediately links with the Elder Folk's culture. But what if there are? What if they have become so familiar it has made them invisible?

As Gooch put it:

The genetic crossing of Cro-Magnon and Neanderthal produced not just (a) highly gifted individuals ('the mighty men of old, the men of renown') but (b) an entirely new species of human — ourselves...[13]

The scarcity of evidence to support his position when Gooch originally began to lay it bare means one must consider the part that intuition likely played in this writer's work. Gooch is not the only person to make this connection between the Elder Folk's very developed cerebellum and its potential to develop a highly attuned sensorium, intuition, and maybe even a more developed emotional intelligence.

To take into account the perspective of another author on this topic here is a lengthy but important quote from James Shreeve's *The Neanderthal Enigma*:

> *The purpose of knowledge, to a Neandertal, would not be to gain control, but to increase intimacy, not just between individuals but between the individual mind and whatever it sees, touches, smells, and remembers. To this end, I imagine Neandertals possessing a different kind of consciousness. The plurality of "selves" we invent to negotiate our guarded social encounters would be a waste of psychic energy for Neandertals. Instead, let's give them a single but infinitely graded ego, an analog self, as opposed to our own digitized identities. The borders between the Neandertal and the Neandertal world are fuzzy. For us, consciousness seems like an inner "I" resting somewhere deep in the mind, eavesdropping on our stream of thoughts and perceptions.*
>
> *This, of course, is neuro-fiction; there is no special center of the brain where consciousness resides. I would give the Neandertals a fictive inner voice, too, but move it out, away from the center, so that it speaks from nearer to that fuzzy border with the world. A Neandertal thought would be much harder to abstract from the thing or circumstance that the thought is about. The perception of a tree in a Neandertal mind feels like the tree; grief over a lost companion is the absence and the loss. Neandertal psyche floats on the surface of the moment, where the metaphor of consciousness as a moving stream is perfect, the motion serene and unimpeded by countercurrents of re-think, counter-think, and double-think.*

I picture two Neandertals sitting side by side, their intimacy so exact that their interior voices cross and coalesce, like two streams merging into a river, their waters indistinguishable.[14]

This last part, where Shreeve speaks of the intimacy where interior voices coalesce, has come very close to describing the kind of dream-sharing experiences that people are capable of that Emma Wilby covered in her book about Isobel Gowdie. Where she showed that people are capable of this kind two streams merging experience, until their waters become indistinguishable. As she puts it:

Through experimental research involving many groups of people over several years, Magallon, Ullman et al. have demonstrated that certain personalities and conditions are conducive to the generation of mutual dreaming than others. First, as with the ability to shamanize, psychological propensity seems to play a role. According to Magallon successful mutual dreamers are 'also likely to have frequent encounters with the "borderlands" between dreaming and waking. In addition to mutual dreams they report experiences with false awakenings, astral projection, lucidity, hypnogogia, trance, and other altered states that are not quite waking, not quite dreaming.' Also interesting, in the context of witch lore, is the fact that successful mutual dreamers [people who share dream experiences] report a higher than average incidence of flying dreams: with an astonishing sixty-one percent ... experiencing mutual dream flight.[15]

It gives us more insight still when Wilby goes on to say that the conditions under which the dreams are shared is significant. This ability for the two streams of consciousness to come together during altered states hangs on the atmosphere generated in the room, types of stimuli used and the relationship between the dreamer and the experiment leader. This points to a kind of emotional logic needed to unlock this part of our Elder Folk ancestor's psyche, one that lays latent in many people and pronounced in those who possess an abundance of the above mentioned qualities. It suggests that there must be certain things achieved to break down the separation of consciousness between people.

Shreeve's vision of what it would be to feel like the Elder Folk, though not made as witchcraft-specific as Gooch's work, asks us to imagine into what it would be like not be trapped inside our Sapien functions at all times. To be less abstracted from the world, so that the sensory life of something becomes the thing itself without a head-story mashed between us and reality. The detail and passion put into this imaginative leap makes you feel almost like Shreeve can access it somehow, as it were in fact still part of him... This sort of imaginal, emotional-intelligence-provoking exercise helps us to imagine what we might call the archaic substrata of the fleshly stories that still exist in Sapiens, and if we are capable of imagining it, this is probably because it lives on inside us.

To really carve out a space for those ancient stories we will have to follow the call of hunger, the call of children abandoned in the woods, along a trail of bread crumbs back through the forest until we find the witch's house, and then taste it. We have listened to authors like David Abrams in books like *The Spell of the Sensuous* tell us about how the truth is right there in our own senses so many of us have stepped out from, or even raised disconnected from, but what would it mean to rediscover our minority ancestors in this way? And to rediscover with them the place where our sensorium can connect with that of others?

What then will we discover lies on the other side of that threshold beyond which the world that seems to be on the outside will suddenly erupt into us? Would this eruption perhaps feel like the flight experience of the *Eternal Sabbat*, where time and space seem to collapse into a sensual cacophony? The type that all those mutual dreamers brought together in Emma Wilby's studies were getting so close to when they set out to bump their dream narratives into other people's? Furthermore, as Wilby suggested, during Isobel Gowdie's life was such a way of being more natural to many than it seems today?

Nearly any trial that sets out to catch heretics or witches will give us some of the material we need to unpack our sorcerous sensorium. We will find cannibalism of some kind, often literal cannibalism, sometimes more subtle kinds like the baby-cooking where the consumption becomes an aspect of healing. There will be sensual relations that break the standard social rules in numerous ways, especially in regards to promiscuity, and maybe incest,[16] age difference, or queer relations. We will find certain signs of mixed gender expression, along with secrecy of some kind including the denial of the gaze, or the right to speak during a ritual, sight may be denied at all via the use of subterranean locations where 'god cannot see'[17], whether through blood being drawn above the breath, or dogs kicking over lights.

The number thirteen, moving backwards or leftward, and maybe even reversing the prayers or actions of the dominant religion might take place. There will be some kind of involuntary bleeding, which may stem from sacrifice or menses, responses to an ugly or bestial appearance, aversions that need to be confronted, the presence of body hair, asymmetry on the body, deformities such as extra nipples or birthmarks or one hairy ear or strange hand. There will often be the profane kiss on the arse, or the eating of some disgusting substance that brings us into the realm of both ritual uncleanliness and pushing beyond it into something outside of both clean and unclean. There will come with all of this some kind of sensation of awe and terror around the breaking of taboo, none of which may be spoken of afterwards.

These narratives that belong at the bedrock of forbidden things seem to have a double life in us still, they are banned and yet fascinating, they draw us to their withered bosom for the witch-milk of forgotten dreams. They possess a power-charge that can create a ritual potency where time and the very sense of the order of things is temporarily turned upside down. This image of inversion is as important as the widdershins circling. When the main prerequisites of a culture are disturbed, where tracks in the land are activated rather than controlled and segregated by the shedding of uncontrollable sorcerous blood, a charged vacuum of power can rush into a new shape — something we might call sorcery.

At such moments the difference we are taught exists between body and spirit is dissolved in a cauldron of black fire, disgust is transformed, sublimated into something before unknown, something that goes beyond delight and disgust. At such moments the long teeth of the Elder Folk begin to grow inside our head, and we learn that they still long to feed and be fed.

As Gooch who could clearly hear the echoes of this happening put it:

A biological supernova occurred when Cro-Magnon and Neanderthal man met. We can, if we will listen, still clearly hear the echoes of that explosion and observe its after-effects... [B]ehind these echoes and tendrils we can also then detect the still fainter traces of Neanderthal civilisation itself, and hear the still fainter echoes of falling cities of dreams.

Notes

1. Norman Cohn, op cit., p.164.
2. Cohn, Ibid., p.227.
3. Gooch, p.2058.
4. This unknown genetic donor has been theorised to be an unknown species or perhaps an early population hangover of homo erectus.
5. McArthur, E., Rinker, D., & Capra, J. Quantifying the contribution of Neanderthal introgression to the heritability of complex traits. 'Nature Communications', 12(1). (2021) doi: 10.1038/s41467-021-24582-y
6. Marion Roach, *Roots of Desire: the myth, meaning and sexual power of red hair.*, Bloomsbury Publishing, (2005).
7. Razib Khan, Ötzi — more Neandertal than the average bear. (2022). Retrieved 14 November 2022, from https://www.discovermagazine.com/health/otzi-more-neandertal-than-the-average-bear
8. Michele Stephen, Witchcraft, Grief, and the Ambivalence of Emotions, American Ethnologist. (1999) 26 (3): pp. 711–737. doi:10.1525/ae.1999.26.3.711. JSTOR 647444.
9. Stephen, Ibid., p.226.
10. Stephen, p.716.
11. Stephens, p.718.
12. Norman Cohn discusses the likelihood of a woman whose mother was burned as a witch being more likely to later be persecuted due to this belief that witchcraft ran in families in Europe on p.266 of *Europe's Inner Demons* for instance.
13. Gooch, op cit., p.39.
14. James Shreeve, *The Neandertal Enigma: Solving the mystery of human origins.*, Penguin Books, (1997).
15. Emma Wilby, *The Visions of Isobel Gowdie: Magic, Witchcraft and Dark-Shamanism in Seventeenth century Scotland*, Sussex Academic Press, (2010) p.508.

This kind of deviancy, including incest, can also be found in the Balinese Layek cultural experience as outlined in Michele Steven's paper. The Waldensians were also accused of this as referenced on p.53 of Norman Cohn's *Europe's Inner Demons*.

16. Cohn, Ibid., p.53.

Chapter 6

Profane Kisses and Ritual Uncleanliness

Once upon a time there was an original profane kiss. As George Bataille put it: 'A kiss is the beginning of cannibalism.' We do not know the details, whether it was between a man and a woman, or same sex people, or perhaps it involved the sharing of a meal? It happened about one-hundred thousand years after the last common ancestor between Sapiens and the Elder Folk lived. During this kiss Methanobrevibacter oralis[1] was passed from the mouth of the Neanderthal into the mouth of the Sapiens, and still thrives there today. Even though the Elder Folk who once developed this micro-organism no longer walk around in their entirety, another type of reproduction still happened, the reproduction of a very small being that still exists in all our mouths today, passing its lineage down even now. Reminding us that none of us are clean in the imagined sense, nor are we meant to be clean.

We are larger organisms upon which smaller organisms live. Though we may attempt to exert some control over some of those organisms, especially during an epidemic, we can never truly be conscious of what requires our flesh as its home, or what is jumping from another body to ours, and copying itself for the next fifty-thousand years. This coincides with the faith of the Good Folk, which was quite remarkably described by Robert Kirk in the 17th century, long before the microscope, it runs as follows:

It is one of their tenets that nothing perishth but moves in a circle, lesser and greater and is renewed and refreshed in its revolutions, as tis another that every body moves (which is a sort of life) and that nothing moves but has another animal moving upon it, and so on, to the utmost minutest corpuscle that is capable of being a receptacle of life.'[2]

Whilst this original kiss happened, with its minutest corpuscles of life being passed between bodies, it might have been witness to some of the intimacy that allowed the hybrid-craft-faith of witchcraft to be planted in the womb. The womb that belonged to the Elder Folk woman we spoke of at the beginning with hair on her chin who pushed that first hybrid child out her cunny. Later in history with one type of human absorbed into the other, like those two streams Shreeve spoke of, with songs of descent, and songs of lands collided, only then can we imagine the growth of the species-wide neurosis of Sapiens searching for the source of contaminant inside their own communities, as a deflection from how they search for this part deemed beastly, that they fear, and deep down know, lives inside themselves also.

The actual kiss of shame, or the devil's kiss, is well known amongst people with an interest in the witchcraft persecutions. Norman Cohn in his *Europe's Inner Demons* links it to the accusation against early Christians that they kissed the genitals of their leader, and there is some connection indeed. Here we must remember the fire believed to emit from the genitals and anus of the Layek in Balinese belief culture, which suggests there may be a double meaning to this act, placing the kiss close to the source of witch-fire. Whilst the location of the kiss is different the intention in the two claims for taboo-intimate-behaviour are the same, as the word shame indicates.

Both accusations whether the kiss was on the genitals or arse were meant to attract our disgust, and they hang on a tradition of ritual uncleanliness and extra emphasised sexuality that links the figure to dehumanisation. Whether the incest or sexual act was linked to Cagot people, Cathars, witches or Layek it seems to repeat its motifs. The idea that something that isn't clean got up amongst us once upon a time, something maybe less (or more) human, something that needs to be exposed, examined by a witch-hunter, searched and driven out... The feeling of contamination exudes from the bans on drinking fountains and places where women's blood is to be allowed to flow.

It isn't until 1180 where we actually hear the Cathars described as kissing a devil on its rear in the form of a cat. The language used by Walter Map is very similar to the mocking tone that described early Christians. He admits that Cathars means 'pure ones', which is true, and puts across a feeling that they themselves believe they are the ones who are 'worthy and pure' even whilst they do these terrible acts.[3]

On the subject of the body and blood of Christ, the blessed bread, they deride us. Men and women live together, but no sons or daughters issue — of the union.[4] Many, however, have dropped their errors and returned to the faith, and these relate that about the first watch of the night, their gates, doors, and windows being shut, each family sits waiting in silence in each of their synagogues, and there descends by a rope which hangs in the midst a black cat of wondrous size. On sight of it they put out the lights, and do not sing or distinctly repeat hymns, but hum them with closed teeth, and draw near to the place where they saw their master, feeling after him, and when they have found him they kiss him. The hotter their feelings, the lower their aim: some go for his feet, but most for his tail and privy parts. Then, as though this noisome contact unleashed their appetites, each lays hold of his neighbour and takes his fill of him or her for all his worth.

This tale holds a lot in common with the Christian heresy we have already visited, especially the inclusion of the putting out of the light. There are a few more details here that are of interest,

75

not necessarily because they are believable but because of what they say about the society that was worried about such things. We noticed the silence of the group, the darkness. The fact that they do not sing or repeat any hymns and instead make a certain sound like a hum through closed teeth, as though in a pre-verbal recognition of the sacred as unspeakable, before feeling around to get a sensory experience of their animal master. Whether this claim was based on anything real or not it shows us something about these dark and non-verbal conditions that seemed so threatening to the religion of the time.

There is a lot of revulsion in this language in Map's testimony and it gets even more graphic with Gregory IX's where he goes into detail about the heretics receiving the tongue and saliva from the toad directly into their mouths during the kissing. Here he gives us a humanised devil figure who could be directly out of the witchcraft persecution, both in term of the coldness of the individual and his ability to remove the glamour cast over the individual by the church.

He is met by a man of wondrous pallor, who has black eyes and is so emaciated thin that since his flesh has been wasted, seems to have remaining only skin drawn over [his] bone. The novice kisses him and feels cold, like ice, and after the kiss the memory of the Catholic faith totally disappears from his heart.[5]

This sort of style of aversion confrontation exists in some expressions of Tantra — a word that interestingly means 'loom, weave, warp'. The path of the Aghori in particular has elements in it that confront and overcome Hindu taboos of all sorts. Panchamakaratantra or the so-called Five M's, involves either symbolically or actually breaking five major taboos as a form of moving beyond aversion. Robert Svoboda describes it in the following way:

The left hand must perform all the inauspicious activities, cleaning the excretory orifices and killing animals... An Aghori forgets the meaning of inauspicious. Orthodox people think that corpses, skulls, and menstrual blood are filthy, and that anyone who would use them for worship is insane or worse. The very thought of eating human flesh nauseates them. But the Aghori finds these things extremely useful to him. To become an Aghori is to see everything in the world as the Atman... The Atman is feeding the Atman to the Atman. When an Aghori reaches this stage he eats whatever he finds dead dogs, slops from the gutter, offal, his own flesh... He sees everything as one, no attraction or revulsion.[6]

This kind of aversion confrontation and overcoming is seen in some Tantric circles as part of mythical attainment. Svoboda talks about waiting beside cremation for the skull to pop in a satisfying manner (or perhaps not satisfying at all because even cannibalism is simply the Atman feeding the Atman to the Atman) exposing the brains which he would then eat. He challenges every form of disgust that humans have, even some that might be linked to disease prevention like faeces and dog-eating, all as an attempt to liberate his experience from the ties of judgmentalism and discrimination.

What we learn from this is that the principle of disgust and the way it links to declaring someone inhuman is very important to our history of cruelty towards one another. If you meditate on how the sensation of disgust impacts your body you will note that it conjures the black-serpent, the influence that pushes something, or someone, away. This force is sometimes there to protect us. It is difficult to overcome the body's desire to move away from a rotting corpse because the smell tells us that it is not good to be around it. The same thing can be said for an open sewer. The fetch moves to protect itself from bacteria and virus-laden environments.

What about when the disgust principle is a bit more far-ranging? Anyone who has been witness to verbally or physical examples of homophobia will know how using terms to provoke distaste about sexual acts deemed to be done by those people is part of the psychology of this way of being. This tactic is powerful enough that some queer people even internalise these ideas about themselves as being physically repulsive. Others reject them as activating to trauma, others embrace them. The Tantric approach, especially the type that is often called left-hand Tantra by English speakers is a path that seeks to embrace and denature these kinds of reactions. In this way it holds a great power.

The witchcraft I know is different to this style of Tantra in some key ways, such as the fact we have a notion of potentially harmful aversions and harmless aversions. Because we honour the fetch we tend to avoid aversions that are generally linked to the possibility for harm to our bodies, all up until we have no choice but to endure that thing, at which point we might start leaning into similar psychological skills as those that Svoboda expressed. Nonetheless, the idea of being able to ride the black-serpent, either with red-serpent power or in other ways, is an important, even a key aspect of the witchcraft that reared me.

There is also some evidence that witchcraft involved psychological conditioning of this kind. One example is where the postulant was sent to kiss the arse of the devil but under his Majesty's tail there turned out to me another face instead of a hole. This reflected a common belief shown in art at the time that humans had faces on the top half because we were designed to look towards god and heaven, but demons were oppositely created. To the witch the message behind this seemed to be that on the other side of one's hesitation to engage in such a carnal act as this might be something that isn't so confronting to begin with. Even when the Devil's Kiss is portrayed as literally on the arse it's important to remember that sexual or sensual activities that involve the anus are non-reproductive, which to Christian minds of the past made them sinful in themselves.

Up until the nineteenth century anal sex was still described (or not described!) as an unspeakable act. For many Catholics the sole thing allowing men and women to enjoy marital sex was the possibility of a baby being born. If that element wasn't present then something devilish was likely already afoot. If one instead views the body from the perspective of witchcraft one would say that the bowel and excretory holes are linked to the Underworld, or perhaps even are the Underworld as manifest in the microcosmic universe of the body. Honouring the devil's arse could indeed be said to have many a deeper meaning.

These considerations around the actual profane kiss aren't the only set of tracks left on the ground in European sources. You only have to look into what other parts or types of bodies we have been disgusted by to find more examples. As such there are numerous tales where the appearance of a figure is considered repulsive in some way, and only the hero who is able to see the different type of beauty that lies beyond what is typically considered ugly is capable of winning the prize. Vargeisa (Wolf-fire), from Nordic tradition,[7] had the hooves of a horse, and the mane and tail as well. Prince Hjálmþér is told he must kiss her to get her help. Instead of being disgusted the response Hjálmþér gives to her oddity is merely to remark: 'you do not seem much like other women to me.' He kisses her without reluctance (probably an important part of the magic) and she transforms into a beautiful maiden.

This story links to a variety of other stories colloquially known as Kissing the Hag, all of them have the same meaning and outcome. Those who will kiss her find themselves blessed. Those who choose to be seen with the supposedly ugly hag by day get to have her as a younger woman by night in their sheets. The test appears to hang around both repugnance and also ego. Like in the Irish tale of Niall of the Nine Hostages[8] where each brother has a kiss demanded of him by a hag described as hideous who guards a well in return for water. Some refuse, one gives a peck that quite frankly wasn't up to her standards. Only Niall kisses her properly. This results not only in him being granted water but the kingship of Ireland, because it turns out that hideous hag was actually the core sovereignty of Ireland... The message here is that things that we consider ugly, things that might even be considered to be examples of ritual uncleanliness can be transmuted by someone who can overcome their sense of aversion to the strange and the different. Here is a kind of witchcraft all its own.

In the world it appears there are two types of uncleanliness. One has its roots in actually disease inducing habits and substances. The other is more arcane. How do we explain the disgust with which older people's bodies are treated? Unless our sole reason for ever engaging in things like kissing is reproduction there really isn't a health-asserting reason for it. Especially considering that finding out a younger person is infertile or has had an operation to prevent conception usually doesn't induce disgust. What then is the mythos around the body of the hag that creates this black-serpent feeling this fear of her growing teeth?

The same reasonable enough questions can be asked about the human body. I have heard it said that if a dog bites a man, and a man bites the dog back that the dog is more likely to be the one to die of an infection from the number of bacteria that the human mouth holds. Assuming both parts are well washed one struggles to understand, in a world full of all types of bacteria floating in the air, including types derived from faeces, why placing the dirtier hole onto what is often a slightly cleaner one is the cause for dehumanisation? All of this requires a little education in modern humans, this idea that our faces are clean to begin with.

Cleanliness as an asserted moral virtue seems to have begun somewhere between the Victorian and the Edwardian period. Diseases abounded and it was no doubt noticed and eventually proven, that those minutest corpuscles of life abounded everywhere. If we test ourselves now we discover we have bacteria, viruses, fungal spores, and all kinds of feral life all over us. We are never anything other than what the Good Folk described us as, larger bodies holding smaller bodies. The challenge is to find ways to keep ourselves and our immune systems able to get them all under control without getting carried off by paranoid ideas that develop into a neurosis. None of us are clean. Nothing that is alive, regardless of what religion, what sexual practices, or what blood-lines it carries, is clean.

We can then view ritual cleanliness as a theory a society has gathered over time about what will keep it safe. Though it's likely that most people don't remember why something is taboo, whether that be the devil's kiss or eating pork, there is no doubt a health-related reason at some point where the aversion begins. As we come to know more about what is harmful, and what is not, hygiene and cooking methods and numerous other preventative measures can be used to keep ourselves free of disease. We now know that other things, such as just breathing in the presence of other people can lead to disease, and our sense of the 'unclean' and what cleanliness actually means, and can mean, can be adjusted accordingly.

Notes

1. Weyrich, L., Duchene, S., Soubrier, J. et al. Neanderthal behaviour, diet, and disease inferred from ancient DNA in dental calculus. Nature 544, 357–361 (2017). https://doi.org/10.1038/nature21674

2. Robert Kirk, The Secret Commonwealth of Elves, Fauns and Fairies., Dover Publications, p.52.

3. Walter Map in his De Nugis Curialium of ~1180.

4. Lack of productivity in baby lives was usually linked to anal sex.

5. Gregory IX Bull Vox in Rama.

6. Robert E. Svoboda, Aghora: At the left hand of god., Sadhana Publishing, p.229.

7. Sandra Ballif Straubhaar, Nasty, Brutish, and Large: Cultural Difference and Otherness in the Figuration of the Trollwomen of the "Fornaldar sögur", Scandinavian Studies 73, No. 2 (Summer 2001), pp. 105-124.

8. T. O'Donovan, Irish Sagas: Echtra mac nEchach Muigmedóin text. (2022) Retrieved 14 November 2022, from https://iso.ucc.ie/Echtra-mac/Echtra-mac-text.html

Chapter 7

Union Sinister

As soon as one begins to scratch away at the abstract geometry scraped into the cave walls shared by Sapiens and before us (also us) the Older Peoples, we become aware of what looks like doubleness and triplicity, unfolding into multiplicity, where dualism becomes dynamism. Of course, it's not actually a real doubleness, it consists of our perceived sense of self that excludes others, and then it contains also those People of the Outside, seen as belonging to a single excluded category. This Otherness is actually a plethora of closely related hominid species breeding back in with each other, with between 1-6% of current human genetic material belonging to them.

It is worth reconsidering Otzi the iceman mummy whose body survived five-thousand-years had about double the Neanderthal genetic material that most Europeans possess today. Given he lived only five thousand years ago we can tell from this that we have lost over half of our Neanderthal genetic material in quite a short time in Europe, with at least one individual having maintained over double the current standard amount for about thirty-thousand years. We can guess that this percentage varied depending on what pressures our species faced and what characteristics were selected for. As Otzi was forced to face an often cold and harsh environment which led to him being preserved in ice the harsh hand of Grandmother Nature might have given precedence to Neanderthal traits over a series of generations. He is not alone on this front, as the Philippine Ayta Magbukon group have at least the same percentage of Denisovan DNA[1] as what Otzi had of Neanderthal, which is very intriguing.

Given that 5-6% constitutes one in twenty of someone's genetically active ancestors being Other this is significant and requires further digging and sorting for us as a so-called species, both practically and emotionally. This digging should be done right into the cremation ground of humankind's primary taboos and rejected zones, even though, like Sugito with Doe, we often don't want to humanise the being we fear we have replaced, stolen land from, oppressed or murdered. What this dig into ourselves and others brings us quickly to is the mythic root-system of the divine twins. This story, involving two deeply connected, usually male individuals (but not always) can be found as a prominent theme in most Indo-European derived cultures. This gives the story a wide range that covers Britain, Ireland, as well as Western, Northern, and much of Eastern Europe, yet the story is wider flung even than that, as we shall see.

Often a powerful testing ground for the dispersal of non-Indo-European cultural elements the Basque region can also be seen to possess its own divine twins — sons of the primary deity Mari — usually named Atxular and Mikelatz. This may or may not point to the idea being older than Indo-European settlement. The standard narrative suggests that Atxular embodies the quintessential Basque soul.[2] He does this with his own kind of internal balancing act. After having learned from the Devil in a church in Salamanca and escaped he becomes a priest, indicating that the Basque soul consists of a revealing balance reached between both holy and diabolic influences.

Mikelatz his twin brother instead seems to have a more feral character and is sometimes associated with the spirit of storms called Hodei, or like many wildman figures in Basque mythology to appear as a young red bull. This bull depiction makes Mikelatz very similar to a story-figure as far away geographically as Enkidu. This story of the two brothers that represent two seemingly opposed aspects of human, and perhaps also in-human, nature can be traced back as far as this first epic to be recorded by humans The Epic of Gilgamesh, where we meet Gilgamesh, the almost too civilised man, who must fight with, come to love in an almost romantic manner, and finally find balance with his partly bestial brother Enkidu, who embodies a form of wild innocence.

This broad geographical extension of the divine-twins (between the Basque province seated between France and Spain and ancient Mesopotamia) should perhaps not surprise us too much. It is true that we can find both Indo-Iranian and Armenian examples of this story-thread. In the Mahabharata epic[3] which treats of divine twins, Nakula is described in terms of his exceptional beauty, warriorship and martial prowess, while Sahadeva is depicted as patient, wise, and thoughtful. The Armenian heroes Sanasar and Baldasar[4] appear as divine twins in the epic tradition, born of princess Tsovinar. Sanasar is more warlike than his brother and finds a horse of fire. In an alternate account, their mother is named princess Saⓞan, who drinks water from a horse's footprint and gives birth to both heroes. This is a noteworthy trail of breadcrumbs for us to follow because this drinking from the horse's print echoes the 'drink to him in a horse's hoof' refrain found in Welsh witchcraft tradition.[5]

It also makes us think of the half-horse woman Vargeisa who was concealing many wonders once her strange appearance was accepted. The horse often makes people think of post-horse-riding, chariot-bearing peoples, but a look at the front teeth of a horse, and the insult 'horsey' we use to describe women of a certain appearance, will make you think of the night of the long teeth. This may or may not link to traditions like that of the Mari Lwyd[6] in Wales where winter and death is represented by a horse-skull ghost. As the witch's sabbath also involves the burning of the horse's skull in Wales and that it is used as a nidding pole is a Norse curse flinging, this could be extra significant.

What then do these horse-son twins represent? The fundamental sense of contrast and what the authors of *The Dawn of Everything* popularised in their use of the term schismogenesis — where two cultures develop around the idea of opposition or even being the literal counter-culture of each other. The divine twins seem to function a bit like this in most Indo-European contexts, but this element doesn't seem quite so simple when we meet the divine-twins in other parts of the world. In Vodou, for example, we encounter them as the Marassa Jumeaux or the divine twins who are served first only after Legba. Whilst a non-initiate can only say certain things about them it is clear that they violate the notion of contrast, for whilst they are two their ultimate number is also three, and whilst they are child spirits they are considered one of the oldest of the lwa, to somehow exist before all the others. One wonders if this lack of contrast, or even lack of binary contrast, has something to do with the fact Africa has the least genetic impact from the Elder Folk and therefore be less likely to react against them?

This liminal space that the twins occupy seems to represent a refusal to ultimately designate negative qualities to one, or create impactful contrast is also to be found in forms of contemporary witchcraft that identify themselves as traditional. One of the reasons this is relevant is that Vodou is considered to be one of the influences upon the Faerie and Feri traditions.[7] Whilst this would have originally happened some time ago it can only be imagined that the influence continues.

Take this quote from a modern initiate:

Typically, one Twin is described as the Blue Bird. This Bird is the loci of the heavenly plane, and is generally pleasant and easy-going. His personality characteristics are those that we humans value highly. The other Twin is seen as a Black Serpent, who may or may not be His Lover. This Serpent is the loci of the earthly plane, and is generally unpleasant and acerbic. His personality characteristics are those that we humans fear most, though He is not evil. Both beings are sacred in their own right. Together, they are most often visualised as a peacock with a serpent twined around his ankle. He is the Winged Serpent, the Blue God, Living Rainbow.[8]

Here we see a more complex and layered telling of a story about darkness and negation. The author goes on to add: 'Together they form the holism that is our human potential and our infinite capacity for both beauty and darkness', thus making it clear that both individuals form part of a necessary whole.

To better knead the clay of this idea in our heads and hands let us look more closely at the Indo-European current, and then what lurks around and beside it. The first thing to be aware of is the very strong link with the horse. There could be more than one reason for this. The first is that the horse and horse-driven battle was a very potent life-style catalyser. People who did things from the back of horses tended to sweep the horseless before them. Of course, the question was more complex and layered. It should not be discounted that the term 'horse' carried some of the meaning for earlier Indo-European peoples as it does in Vodou — i.e.: recognising the human as vessel for the spirits.

Having the horse to go off allows us to put a rough date on the earliest fracturing of the story, to see things as related to horse riding and the use of war chariots. Similar to the age of Otzi, horse riding and milking seems to have started about five thousand years ago. The other more important theory about what happened at this time was the introduction of Indo-European languages into Europe, carried upon the tongues of settlers. It was a busy time, especially to be a horse! Somewhere deeper into the fibres of this nest of stories there is another animal lurking, one with big eyes all the better to see you with. To engage the wolf we will need to knock upon the door of Odin and Loki. In the poem *Lokasenna* or 'Loki's Flyting' which consists of a verbal joust between Loki and the other gods the relationship between the two of them is framed like this:

> *Do you remember, Odin, when in bygone days*
> *we mixed our blood together?*
> *You said you would never drink ale*
> *unless it were brought to both of us.*[9]

This lets us know that Odin and Loki are blood brothers who have once been very close. This is reminiscent of the brotherly, yet almost romantic, love that exists between Gilgamesh and Enkidu, where we find examples like this one that discusses mourning:

> *But his* [Enkidu's] *eyes do not move,*
> *he touched his heart, but it beat no longer.*
> *He covered his friend's face like a bride,*
> *swooping down over him like an eagle,*
> *and like a lioness deprived of her cubs*
> *he keeps pacing to and fro.*[10]

The frequent references to marriage and strong emotion often make it unclear whether some kind of romantic element exists in these connections. This can be cross referenced with our Feri initiates claim that the darker twin 'may or may not be his lover', if he is not then the emotion is as strong as if he was. It's inevitable this topic will come up in witchcraft because everybody initiated by the same person becomes brothers and sisters to one another. This liminal quality to the relationship ties into the fact that in Haitian Vodou the twins are also triplets, they are two boys, two girls, one boy and one girl, and none of these are viewed in terms of contradiction.

Odin brings up that Loki spent eight winters beneath the earth as a woman milking cows, and during this time gave birth to children. Loki retaliates by pointing out that Odin had practiced the type of sorcery known as Seidhr which is considered perverse, womanly and being 'ridden'. Loki spends a lot of time breeding divine animals during his transformations and is considered to be the parent of the wolf-father. Most importantly he has been involved in being female during reproduction animal transformation, not just human, as he was the mare with the stallion that bred Odin's eight-legged horse Sleipnir.

In the Fourth Branch of the *Mabinogi* we observe the brothers Gwydion and Gilfaethwy exchange words in a way that suggests one of the greatest acknowledgments of emotional intimacy observable in the Mabinogion. We see Gwydion consistently refer to his brother as 'my soul', but due to Math's powers to hear discourse on the wind, he must also observe Gilfaethwy well enough to guess at what is wrong, suggesting a deep emotional understanding between them. When Gilfaethwy in a roundabout way admits he longs for the virgin Goewin whose job it is to anchor their uncle Math in the nourishing powers of sovereignty, Gwydion immediately undertakes action. He plans how they might bring about the situation to allow his brother to physically access the girl. There is nothing of romance in this tale that is for certain, but Goewin seems to represent more than a mortal girl, like Niall's hag she is also sovereignty, though it is not inarguable that she is also simple a girl as well.

In punishment for overstepping of Goewin's will leading to her rape, and the unsettling of Math's dominion over the land, the two brothers are punished in a similar way to how Loki produced animal offspring. Gwydion and Gilfaethwy are forced to commit incest by being changed into beasts by Math, presumably one of each sex. It is implied they are not in control of the sinister incestuous, and same-sex, gender-swapping union they must have then committed. Firstly they are changed into a deer and a stag, they are kept in this condition until they breed a child. Then they are turned into pigs. This is an evocative choice because the sow had certain connotations within Welsh sorcery, and was a druidic animal of some import to the extent that druids were sometimes referred to as little pigs. It is only at the end, when it comes the wolf transformation where we see the ultimate underlaying bestial nature that befits the theft of will they committed, revealing the wolf under the surface. Just as with the other two human-animal people Gwydion and Gilfaethwy's wolf son is called Bleiddyn, and baptised by Math.

There is a certain ghost of a suggestion here that these three partly human, partly animal, children are the embodiment of some alien element of the Othered that has crept in via the influence of unbridled lust of the brothers for Goewin, or perhaps the sovereignty of place that she likely also points towards. As if lust for union with the land reawakens the animal within. Math may have given names and baptism to each of these children but this feral quality lingers.

After leaving a paw print here we must explore the nature of the Celtic werewolf, especially in Ireland and Wales where it is far more ambitious than some other strands of the tale.

In Lady Wilde's work[11] a farmer named Connor goes looking for some lost cows only to discover a family of werewolves. It should attract our attention that as the conversation progresses 'the hag' who is the mother of the grown sons has teeth that seem to become longer while they speak, suggesting either that she is becoming more powerful or half transformed into a wolf. "Wait," says one of the young men when Connor becomes angry. "We are fierce and evil, but we never forget a kindness." This is a clear position on their temperament, because what follows is a story where Connor removed a thorn from a wolf cub's paw and that animal was the young man before him. When he gets home he discovers that the wolf has got him some new cows and helped out at his farm.

Another story from Ireland[12] tells of how a man had a wolf stuck in his back wound 'up to the shoulders'. This tale has a resonance about it of the hollow back sometimes ascribed to The Hidden Folk. This is not the only connection with wider folklore, as we find that when it came to the body of the werewolf[13] while they quit their bodies to go out as wolves their body wasn't to be removed or interfered with. An injunction of this nature against moving the body during 'flight' was also discussed by the Thiess the werewolf from Livonia on the Baltic Sea during the witch trials, and was an idea also understood to exist among the Benandanti that Carlo Ginzberg explores in his books.

In Wales we find the same focus on bloodlines and families of wolf people as was popular in Ireland. Here though we find more detail than the long teeth of the hag-wolf mother, we find a whole distinct appearance to the families known as The Wolves. The way Marie Trevelyan describes it is evocative:

A small farm in Breconshire was occupied by a tenant whose ancestors had the reputation of being remarkable ugly and very eccentric. The man himself had exceedingly pointed and hairy ears and his seven children inherited this peculiarity.[14]

Here we might find ourselves wondering if these Wolves were mythically descended from Bleiddyn? Or remembering the one hairy and strangely shaped ear of the Cagot. Welsh lore also agrees with the general feeling on the continent that a werewolf can be identified by their eyebrows meeting in a point near the bridge of the nose.[15] This characteristic was something given special attention by Stan Gooch, who pointed out that this emphasis on eyebrow hair, or even eyebrow prominence could relate to the strong brow-ridge to be found in the People of the Outside who he connected with the Elder Folk's facial structure. This is something that could be said for the stereotype of the wicked witch's face shape with her hooked nose and deep set eyes as well.

In Wales we find a direct connection between witches and werewolves, with the farm previously having belonged to The Wolves being left in a barren state where all things were blighted. As this has nothing to do with the effect wolves have in the wild[16] we are pressed to link this notion of blight with witchcraft. Also, witches were seen as able to transform men into werewolves at will. This transformation was believed to be for three, seven, or nine days or as many years.[17] We will encounter these numbers quite frequently while exploring these twisted paths. It is worth noting that animals are seen as our brothers and sisters too, and that fusion between man and animal parts is its own kind of sinister union.

These are numbers 3,7, 9, and, of course, 13 often take on a particular importance in witchcraft, and ones that Gooch also makes note of as signs of the Elder Folk's influence. To cause the man to turn into a werewolf the Witch of Wenvoe need only twist her girdle and hide it upon the threshold and here we see that werewolfism like witchcraft is contagious from the woman's body, whose will is made manifest through her spinning and weaving of things like a girdle which is in turn worn on her body, to that of the body of a man. The husband and wife must step over when entering their house after the wedding. The girdle only influences the man.

The power of the witch's girdle as a woven item is a specific area of enquiry we will address again later in this book when we look at weaving and fate. To restore him to human shape the witch needed to throw a charmed lamb skin over his body which seems to work through the Christ-like association of the lamb. It also has the implication there are only two types of man alive in the world at that time, those governed by the wolf, and those by the lamb.

In Livonia we find the most famous of werewolves having been caught and put to trial. He was known as Thiess. To his way of thinking his werewolf brethren and himself were conscripted through no choice of their own and were brought in via contagion, after someone breathing over a drink they shared with the man. They may have also been born in a caul and later confirmed to fight for the Virtue of the wheat and fertility of the land against black sorcerers described as witches. Depending on whether they could steal the wheat seeds back from Hell there would be terrible scarcity in the land. Thiess claimed to be able in his wolf-form to outrun the hounds of hell who worked on the other side of the battle. In Ireland and Wales we had ambitious wolves, here we have virtuous ones, even if they did sometimes capture and slaughter pigs.

Cannibalism and attacks on the body and blood of humans or wild animals is a trait we find in the werewolf almost wherever it appears. They represent and also manifest a yearning in our psyche for the uncivilised that is often at least half unwelcome. As Tom Hiron's *Sometimes a Wild God* says:

...when the wild god arrives at the door you will probably fear him. He reminds you of something dark you might have dreamed. Or the secret you do not wish to be shared.

As elsewhere, Welsh werewolves were believed to most enjoy eating the flesh of young children or maidens as it contains a full lifetime's worth of potential, life-forces, and joy.

Rather than eating the flesh they are described, in Wales, much like a vampire, as sucking the blood until death ensues. This incursion into the lore of the vampire gives extra meaning to the: what large teeth you have! All the better to eat you with is said back to Little Red Riding Hood, giving an extra potency to the appetite for fat and foist, and the long teeth they share with witches, and also our lost cousins and forebears, the Older Peoples.

What is perhaps most important when looking at sibling-hood is that we understand all the layers of it. It could be a fusion between human and fetch animal, where those are the siblings who are 'incestuous'. It could be the kind of family you choose, or that chooses you through your similitude, those who are Marked and hold witch-blood. The divergent, those who are aligned with the wild instead of the tame. Being brothers and sisters is more than simply being biological siblings, it is being blood-siblings with our sworn family.

It is making sorcerous connections with others that challenge us to balance out the extremes in ourselves and our witch-kin, by proving powers that complement their own and push us towards the Mastery of Wholeness. The fetch-mate is another kind of twin-figure with whom the witch is sexually active. Through mysteries that cannot be spoken of here they are joined to us since early times, we are part of each other's puzzle, we solve the riddle of each other, helping to tell the story of each other's throwing bones, to create a diviner's story from the pattern they form. When brother/sister, brother/brother, or sister/sister connections are deemed to be holy this is often the secret behind the claim.

This being said, other than cannibalism, necrophilia and bestiality there are few taboos that upset the majority of Sapiens as much as incest does. The early Christians were accused of these sinister unions, as were the Cagots, and a range of heretics. For such a widely spread rule the breaking of it is also alarmingly common, with a large number of sexual abuse of children accusations having an element of incest about them. For this reason incest can be placed next to menstruation in women as something that is of deep interest to many, and yet is very negatively thought of in a wide range of cultures.

Of course, like a lot of these things that humans forbid but also do, incest is given high standing in cultures where total power and prestige belongs to a particular family. It is almost as if, once feeling a bit above the rules for others, we get to see what some people secretly think about. The current royal family of the UK has a number of cousin-marriages in its history, and this was even more pronounced in cultures that believe in the personal Virtue of certain bloodlines, something we can find in both the Egyptian dynastic system, that of the Incas, and that of indigenous Hawaii, where only highly ranked people were allowed to marry family members. This suggests that the behaviour falls into a queer sort of category, one that is both off-putting and of great interest to others, maybe even at the same time.

Of course, that is only the explanation that reason is capable of tendering. Other explanations take us back around to the importance of refining blood lines that were believed to include the blood of gods, or the Watchers. As mentioned above there is a certain kind of lust for blood with Witch Fire present in it, and this often leads to people with no interest in sex with outsiders who do not possess it. One can only imagine that in belonging to a family with such a history behind it that it might take on a different imaginal tone. For those of us who might belong to families quite different to this, as most of us do, it is somewhat harder to contemplate. What is far easier to contemplate is the way blood-brother pairings can become eroticised. When we encounter our Enkidu and Gilgamesh blood-brother pairings, there is often an intense devotion between these two very different men, one that could be described as almost romantic in its intensity and certainly pushes them both towards a greater Wholeness. In the beginning Gilgamesh is arguably insane with the untethered use of his own power and social invulnerability. After meeting and being tempered by Enkidu he becomes something far more decent.

Same sex incest is something not often considered when the topic of this taboo comes up, as the only real (as in, physical non-mythological) reason to forbid incest between two adults is the possibility of inherited problems in any children born of a union. It is perhaps important that as the Feri initiate said, these twins may or may not be lovers. There is a veil of mystery, a denial of the gaze of the uninitiated around this connection where it is important that we do not actually know for sure. There are different degrees of incest in mythology, things from in-laws, through to cousins, brothers and sisters and even occasionally parents and children. It occurs in mythology of many nations.

Occasionally this kind of thing is available as a privilege to gods but not to humans. In the Ynglinga Saga it tells of how brother-sister marriages were traditional among the Vanir, the pre-Aesir gods of the Norse religion. This gives the indication that incest was part of some older way of doing things that is no longer acceptable, considered primitive, and maybe just not a great idea for our species that already lacks genetic diversity. In British mythology we find this same presence of incestuous urges emerging among the elder race that preceded the gods of the current people.

In the Welsh sources these are known as the broadly as The Children of Llyr, but this term only makes reference to the royal line. A dispute of some kind between Llyr and Euroswyd results in Euroswyd becoming the father of twins to Penarddun, who is a daughter of Beli and Ana/Don. Here we are enmeshed in the story of the twins as opposing forces, but this time one of them, Efnisien, ascribes to behaviours deemed forbidden by society, whilst Nisien's heart holds nothing but goodness.

The second and third Branches, in various different ways, identify the close association between incest/endogamy and internecine violence — these tendencies being most vividly represented by the savagely psychopathic Efnisien, whose primitive jealousy towards his own sister is expressed in a murderous hostility to her husband and his offspring.[18]

It perks up the ears of the keen listener that this jealousy Efnisien is feeling towards his sister Branwen is described as primitive, seeming to reenforce the idea that there is something pre-civilised about the impulse.

Overt aversion towards sexual contact with family members may or may not be natural for Sapiens, and certainly most people claim to feel it. In the current world population where our genome is already less various than that of two different Chimpanzee troops, the idea still has a confused history. As is quite well-known, Freud theorised a form of aversion that would eventually form around the idea of sexual relations inside a family. During childhood before the rules were fully learned, that boys naturally desired their mothers and wished to supplant their fathers, and that girls desired their fathers.

This information, released into the world by Freud who had access to the secret fantasy life of his patients seemed to suggest to humans that some sort of hidden world existed for all people, one where the rules of society were more porous than in reality, one they might have casually related to the unconscious or subconscious mind. One can only imagine how this changed people's perception of their lives and those of others around them. Knowing it was not them alone who was subject to such outside-the-box thoughts and fantasies exploding in many directions. This was something which must have done a lot for the self-concept of a lot of people.

Since then a lot has been and would be said in theory circles about the heteronormativity of Freud's theory and how well it would apply to non-middle class people of non-European origin? This reflects different key anxieties in our age to his. Far more disturbing again than the racial and class specificity of his 'people are like this' tale, is that Freud had the opportunity to be the champion of abused children when he gathered a lot of reports of adult-child incest. The paper received a negative response towards his research that claimed to uncover the prevalence of adult-child incest so he pulled the paper and came up with a theory that children fantasise that adults do such things to them.

The idea that girls desiring their fathers and boys desiring their mothers could be an example of Freud gaslighting victims into being the one who wanted the act is a dark place to explore. This high number of abused children was relevant primarily to bourgeois, Viennese society at the time, nonetheless, the presence of this adult-child incest tells us one or two things about the prohibition, and the reality of the behaviours people actually perform. What can't be denied is that what Freud discovered about people helped to reinforce that there was a great deal of activity, or at the extreme least, ideation, fantasy, and impulse that his patients were not able to talk about in the outside world, insights that he got to see as their therapist. The way he as therapist was able to twist that finding when it won him no hearts is also revealing.

Unlike the priest who during confession would hand out punishments for people's outside-the-box actions or thoughts, in psychotherapy moral judgment was tacitly withheld. In practice this was honoured, all up until one needed to decide whether to blame the child or the adult for unwanted incest. The information was absorbed apparently more in the name of understanding than punishing, which one must say revolutionised our understanding of human consciousness. It revealed how much is hidden in a person, and how it was possible to observe some of that content in the right setting without punishing them.

Carl Jung was probably closer to understanding how that toxic material in the subconscious, blamed by each person who thought they alone were a pervert, could become the brewing ground for projection and persecution of others.

If you place what was discovered in psychotherapy about fantasies and urges with what Professor Kinsey uncovered later about actual human sexual practices and fantasies it is easy to see that there is a dark zone to the human psyche. This hidden dimension to the self that by its nature is hidden because it does not fit with the dominant story of civilisation is likely the cook-pot where our witchcraft is brewed and seethed. Kinsey's work also uncovered a lot of confessions to infidelity and incest. Modern authors like Christopher Ryan in his *Sex Before Dawn* have then taken that material, mingled it with what we know about the sexually avid Bonobo-chimpanzee and tried to tell a new story.

By opening up disciplines for studying this hidden life modern psychoanalytic thinkers gave us the very materials we would need to reflect upon the dual-seeming nature of modern Sapiens, a language with which to speak about what might be shadows, or perhaps back-to-front reflections, of hidden ancestors who lived by different social rules and did not necessarily share all our taboos. This kind of thinking is going to be very necessary for talking about the power of conscious violation of rules of behaviour. Some could be as simple as walking backwards rather than forwards, moving leftward rather than rightward, some might be a bit more confronting, depending who the audience is.

Incest is a curious example because whilst most people will attest to a species of disgust when the idea is brought up any understanding of pornography statistics[19] will show that many people don't genuinely feel this disgust, or (and I lean in this direction) the bulk of them enjoy fantasising about things they have no desire to do in real life, or that do in other contexts invoke disgust.[20] Whilst such a position could sound like rule breaking for the sake of itself I believe this kind of behaviour shows us more than this about human nature. Why is it, after all, that we as a species take such an interest in taboo violation for its own sake? To claim we do so is not itself an explanation for why we do.

People exercise certain uncivilised feelings in the practice of BDSM, for instance, where consensual arrangements are reached to pretend to do things they would not want to happen in real life. This can include using words such as daddy to describe a more dominant participant and seems to suggest that Sapiens as a species needs to find means to exercise as well as attempt to exorcise Other material in the psyche. A popular one of these scenes in what might be called adult games involves consensual non-consent. Such an idea is impossible to recreate in real life because you cannot consensually experience non-consent, you can only pretend to experience it. For many this kind of play-acting has some kind of sorcery to it that can help some people to work through fears, to unleash shame, and to create a feeling of power during the experience.

This brings us to the threshold of the idea there is something in the control that kind of play gives the victim that is healing. It makes us consider a both/and approach to taboos, rather than just a banning of them. Where they can be off the table in one's real life — potentially where adult consent is offered they might not be — but still a subject of fantasy or role-play. The notion that adults can play is one that is overwrought by a great deal of suppressed material for so many, yet it is still possible. This seeming contradiction where pretending to lose power can make a person feel more powerful suggests a doubleness to human thinking. This is part of how the tragic genre works too, and modern horror stories. The idea is just a given in society that no one wants to be in the situation the victim is in,. Yet we get something mysterious out of the playing out of it, of watching others enduring it. Part of us needs to discharge animal potency in some way. The tragic genre, historical war movies, folk horror, and standard slasher gore horror, all offer a particular part of the population their release. As does sport for some others.

There are numerous things that are agreed upon boundaries and rules that we agree to avoid in everyday life, yet at the same time there is something primitive in us, something related to the Bonobo's flexible sexual expressions, something that maybe existed prior to those taboos that requires the release of play access to those energies. Maybe this is because there are rules against those things they gain power via repression as Freud might have claimed, or perhaps to gain agency through engaging in some kind of healing confrontation with the feared activity. Or maybe the endorphins released by pain and playing with fear become the instigator?

This, of course, does not mean that all practitioners of BDSM are abuse victims looking to play out their trauma in a more empowered way, it simply means that the traumas of our society are shared, not individual. Girls, for instance, who have been told they would be raped if they strayed from certain behaviours as children might have something imaginative to play out just based of the violence of these ideas that were introduced into their life when they were too young to process them.

The reason people seem to have trouble with understanding why someone who would never actually want to have sex with their own immediate family, might play at incestuous roles is partly because we do not conceive of adults as capable of play. Everything an adult does is seen as very serious and the few taboos that stretch right across our society are considered serious indeed. Perhaps they would explode into less examples of non-consensual incest if they were simply laughed at and or even played with rather than creating such outcry?

Sex is considered such a very serious topic by Sapiens and our lack of relaxation with it is probably a large part of why so many of us struggle to enjoy it properly. Killing is also a serious topic, yet when children pretend to sword fight each other we don't imagine that the child really wishes to kill that other child.

When it comes to endogamy (sex with those from within the group) in the Elder Folk's culture we do have a decently high number of examples of their DNA showing incestuous pairings.[21] Whilst it's possible this had something to do with living in small groups with equally (comparatively)small numbers of their people being alive at the time, we have no way of knowing what the social taboos were when it comes to incest. This being said we have found a number of examples of incestuous parents from the remains of our Elder Folk predecessors, maybe more than one would expect if it was purely a matter of low numbers.

If we are to follow Stan Gooch's approach and consider that anything which modern Sapiens has a particularly strong aversion to is something that belonged to the people we all originally supplanted, or absorbed, we might see traces of some inter-species schismogenesis, or what one might call opposite-copying. We could speculate that incest was less taboo amongst the Elder Folk's culture than it is in Sapiens. The key to this rusty old lock seems to be that we have this taboo for same-sex couples also, who are certainly not going to produce any radically deformed infants. If schismogenesis can be blamed for the very strong feeling most Sapiens have towards same-sex, adult aged, consensual situations, then these taboos that are also strangely intriguing to humans are not merely interesting because they're not allowed, for it doesn't appear that all forbidden behaviours are all equally absorbing.

There are a great deal more people interested in pornography involving step-mothers and their sons than they are about watching people eat shit, as mentioned by our Aghori author, for example. Both are examples of ritual uncleanliness taboo behaviours, but the group size with an interest in one taboo is quite significantly smaller.[22] What this may suggest is that we experience a sliding scale of harm avoidance when it comes to human taboo. The physical effects of eating shit might be considered to be more violent and immediate than the long term family weaknesses that can develop in family groups as a result of repeated incest,[23] especially considering there is no actual blood-tie with a step-member of a family. When it comes to pregnancy even the effects upon children don't seem to fully account for our violent opposition to physically harmless forms of incest between consenting adults.

Unless a predisposition for a recessive gene that is harmful exists, even in a brother and a sister who become pregnant together, it is highly likely that the baby to be little different to any other child. Of course, if that baby then grows up to also marry someone from the same family line then the possibilities of weaknesses developing in the family increases as time goes by, regardless of the stock. As one can observe from watching the outcome of royal family births where cousins have married a good number of times over the years. Even in cultures such as Egypt where incest was encouraged among royals it did seem to take some time of repeating this behaviour before deformity or ill-health emerged.

To work out at the time that incest was the cause of these misfortunes would require a decent sample number of humans to observe whether there was more chance of hereditary problems being passed down due to inbreeding, and also a goodly opportunity to avoid the behaviour. As all inbred children don't appear with immediate monster syndrome the intense disgust with which most Sapiens views incest, whilst at the same time seeming to be mythologically and pornographically obsessed with it, is suggestive there may be other reasons we wish to suppress the thought of it so much, and yet are haunted by wanted to poke at the sea rubble at the same time.

What this brings us to is a conclusion no less radical than Stan Gooch's, yet grounded now in more evidence and a less racist worldview, that what might be called foundation taboos of Sapiens (the things that really stimulate our most uncomfortable yuck feelings) could involve a vigorous rejection of the social mores of one or more species of human that came before us. This love-hate relationship with concepts like incest and cannibalism, that produce very strong knee-jerk reactions in people, ones of both fascination and disgust that can float entire television shows or movies, may in fact speak to a certain doubleness, or triplicity in our nature.

Those Others were Neanderthals to those of a European background, and Denisovans as well in other parts of the world. It is likely the cultural norms of these two species were different from each other, yet maybe more closely related to each other's than to ours. This, of course, is just a guess based around common sense, in that it is somewhat de-humanising to suggest that unlike ourselves a whole species might be exactly the same all around the world, or entirely similar to another species. We can also make the same kind of educated guess that, like the culture of Sapiens, the spread of cultures amid Neanderthal and Denisovan people could have been just as diverse across the globe as our world today. Given that we have experienced royal lines in Egypt and Hawaii, just to name two, who have not been disgusted by endogamy. So, an Altai Neanderthal could have been significantly different to an Asian Neanderthal, with a whole different culture behind them.

It is possible though that the meeting between the groups may have happened early in Sapien development, possibly even before we separated off in as many directions as Fate has taken our brothers and sisters today. We cannot know the character of that meeting only how genetics were shared. Kissing probably happened fairly early on. This suggests there was some thorough admixture. Yet at some point in this story something shifted enough that this part of ourselves became taboo and became associated with forbidden magic. For some people around the world this was a mixing of three main groups over time, something that introduced variants into the DNA in areas highly susceptible to copy number changes,[24] and was perhaps necessary to make Sapiens excel in wonderful and dangerous ways.

Whilst understanding how this happened seems impossible even with scientific input, luckily there is currently more Neanderthal DNA alive than ever before in history, due to the large number of Sapiens that carry it. Via understanding how we work, it is possible to try to approach a manual for how to best use our hybrid brain-heart-guts. This is something of interest to both magical practitioners, people who specialise in this subject, and those just interested in hacking their own biological software for better outcomes.

It is also possible to see things like witch-marks that the inquisitors looked for, and covens give one another, as a lot like the Cagot's goosefoot mark under the left arm, a signal of Otherness. A witch-mark might be a predisposition for psychic experience, as a sign that the hybridity is pronounced in an individual. Whatever someone may think of the idea of experiencing and trusting in the existence of the supernatural realm, we cannot deny how common it is in Sapiens. These qualities we will analyse in more detail as we weave together what is possible to know, what is possible to sense, and consider whether it is in fact the non-human parts of Sapiens that gives us intuition, as Gooch suspected? Or was it more likely something that happened in the hybrid act which creates the figure of the witch as The Person of the Outside?

Notes

1. M. Larena, et al, Philippine Ayta possess the highest level of Denisovan ancestry in the world. Current Biology, 31(19), (2021) 4219-4230.e10. doi: 10.1016/j.cub.2021.07.022.

2. Gallop, op cit., p.166.

3. The Sampradaya Sun – Independent Vaisnava News – Feature Stories, July 2006. (2022). Retrieved 14 November 2022, from https://www.harekrsna.com/sun/features/07-06/features360.htm

4. James Russell, Magic Mountains, Milky Seas, Dragon Slayers, and Other Zoroastrian Archetypes. Bulletin of the Asia Institute, 22, pp.57–77. http://www.jstor.org/stable/24049235.

5. Mari Trevelyan, *Folklore and Folk-Stories of Wales.*, chapter 16, Retrieved 14 November 2022, from https://www.amazon.com.au/Folklore-Stories-Wales-Marie-Trevelyan/dp/0854099387

6. David Howel, Contemporising Custom: the re-imagining of the Mari Lwyd – Research Repository. (2022). Retrieved 14 November 2022, from https://eprints.glos.ac.uk/5861/

7. It is noteworthy that there is a split in this tradition with some initiates who do not believe in teaching their tradition for money calling themselves Faerie.

8. Anaar, Originally published in Witch Eye, Volume 10, Divine Twins, the dual divine force of the Feri Tradition, (2022). Retrieved 14 November 2022, from http://feritradition.org/grimoire/deities/divine_twins.html

9. Harriet Soper, Echoing Retorts in Hárbarðsljóð and Lokasenna. Scandinavian Studies 94(4), (2022) pp.475-503. https://www.muse.jhu.edu/article/869134.

10. Tablet 8, The Epic of Gilgamesh.

11. Lady Wilde, *Ancient Legends, Mystic Charms and Superstitions.*

12. Thomas Rolleston, *Myth and Legend of the Celtic Race*, 1911.

13. George Henderson, *Survival in Belief Amongst Celts*, 1911.

14. Marie Trevelyan, *Folk-Lore and Folk-Stories of Wales*, p. 189.

15. Ibid, p.190.

16. I'm thinking here of the reintroduction of wolves into the Yellowstone national park and the way it encouraged flourishing amongst other species.

17. op cit, p.190.

18. https://mabinogion.info/math.htm

19. Gareth May, Why is Incest Porn So Popular? https://www.vice.com/en/article/8gdz8k/why-is-incest-porn-so-popular-332

20. Kutz I. (2005). Revisiting the lot of the first incestuous family: the biblical origins of shifting the blame on to female family members. BMJ (Clinical research ed.), 331(7531), 1507–1508. https://doi.org/10.1136/bmj.331.7531.1507

21. L. Ríos, et al. Skeletal Anomalies in The Neandertal Family of El Sidrón (Spain) Support A Role of Inbreeding in Neandertal Extinction. Sci Rep 9, 1697 (2019). https://doi.org/10.1038/s41598-019-38571-1

22. Gert Martin Hald, What Types of Pornography Do People Use and Do They Cluster? Assessing Types and Categories of Pornography Consumption in a Large-Scale Online Sample. The Journal Of Sex Research. (2022) Retrieved from https://www.tandfonline.com/doi/abs/10.1080/00224499.2015.1065953

23. The L. Rios article cited two above covers the actual rates at which endogamy is likely to cause harm.

24. David W. Radke, et al, Purifying selection on noncoding deletions of human regulatory loci detected using their cellular pleiotropy, Genome Research, 31, 6, (935-946), (2021).

Chapter 8

Divergent: Evolutionary Chaos Theory

David Graeber and David Wengrow's *The Dawn of Everything: a new history of humanity*[1] we are given the opportunity to explore some of the exceptions to the standard stories the academy holds about world cultures. We hear about cultures where women were declared to be men because it is simply convenient to grant those rights to a person who continues to act like one. There are also people who engaged in obsessive arranging of shells and were therefore believed to be some kind of eccentric sage, individuals in the tribe being only active at night and unable to change this behaviour, unconventional sexual practices, cross dressing,[2] and physical anomalies that would otherwise be classed as deformities have been given some kind of integral place in the group.[3]

These examples of Otherness and difference from a variety of Sapien groups are likely to be examples of what we would now call neurodivergence, or autism, ADHD, and a variety of other behavioural or cognitive differences. Graeber and Wengrow show in their book how some cultures have made them sacred, rather than made them witches. Whatever story we attach to aberrant behaviour changes how other people treat the members of that group, as we can see from the way that punitive laws against witches, Christians, or the Cagots impacted the quality of life of those groups. It is remarkable under the circumstances that we have not been more conscious until recently of the impact that such dangerous storytelling has on people's lives.

Autism in particular is a series of qualities usually considered by neuro-typical people to be anti-social. Though we don't know anywhere near enough about its genetic origins it has been linked in theory to Densovian[4] and Neanderthal heritage.[5] It is natural that we would ask such questions as these Elder Folk were a different kind of human, and it is common amongst neurodiverse people to feel a sense that there is something alien about themselves in relation to neurotypicals, something that leads to them not fitting in. There is sometimes a kind of talent towards specialisation in a topic of extreme interest to be found among people with this diagnosis, a level of focus that has doubtlessly led to numerous breakthroughs in technology and art for Sapiens as a whole.

When it comes to the genetic picture it is likely that only Sapiens exhibited autism as we know it today, and that the gene variations associated with it could in fact derive from the same genetic diversity that gifted our variety-challenged species with enough mutation-enriched parts of our genome to people the whole world with seeming diversity. Of course, this diversity is an illusion, and as has been previously mentioned there is actually less difference between any of us Sapiens than there are between two troops of Chimpanzees, which makes a laughing stock of the neurotic symptom we currently call racism.

In a nutshell, autism results from the highly variable parts of our genome that often help to give Sapiens its edge via mutations. This being said, many people on the spectrum are not perceived to be gifted in a way that is rewarded by late capitalism. It's also possible we wouldn't have those diversity-strands with their extra genetic surprise package that recombines or doubles segments of its genome if it wasn't for our Neanderthal and Denisovan ancestors.[6] You might say that those contributions in question, along with being responsible for a great deal of our genetic diversity, act a bit like a form of hybrid vigour in gifting Sapiens with more variety. Yet what they bring to the table is chaotic, the ultimate mixed genetic bag of possibilities. Some of these gifts have been exceedingly useful, some of them have gifted us our best mathematicians, artists, code-breakers, musicians and archeologists. Others have given us auto-immune diseases and seasonal affective depression and to have possibly gifted us in our hyper variable genetic regions with some of the materials connected to forms of neurodiversity.

A posthumous claim of ND (neurodiversity) may well be put forward for the psychologist and Neanderthal obsessive Stan Gooch. If one includes his other fixation with the idea that the academy rejected his work, which seems to have been an ongoing bugbear for him, one that he could not leave alone like it were an ulcer in his mouth, one can easily recognise him as having most likely been ND. This would also explain why he wasn't embraced and why he struggled to work out the right social cues when it came to picking up the signs that the current attitude towards racism was changing over his lifetime. One almost feels his unpopularity as a serious scholar, despite his qualifications in psychology, has as much to do with basically being someone of a difficult temperament as it did anything else.

With his connection between the Elder People and witchcraft you'd expect him to have risen to greater prominence in occult reading circles. Yet although he lived into an era where you would have expected him to have become conscious particularly of the racism inherent in some of his ideas which he no doubt grew up with, there is no evidence he picked up on these cues or tried to change. The frantic sense of the crucial importance of his topic of interest and his barely masked disdain for the fact other people were not, in his eyes, giving his obsession appropriate attention, is all very recognisable to someone like myself who has parented an ND child.

From our moment in history we are now able to appreciate a sense of Gooch's likely ND status, to consider that when thinking him and his contribution to the topic might help us to overlook some of his eccentricities. We might also consider the intuitive boon he may have obtained from his connection to this topic. There are a few forbidden paths, many quite crooked and overgrown, that draw us to this subject. Some of them can be supported by studies in other disciplines and others have to be filed under the heading Gut Knowing. It is clear to anyone reading through Gooch's material that he was driven by something falling into this latter category, as well as some solid material from the world of reason that he used to support the former.

What this opens up is the tantalising question, more so than an answer, of whether our ancestors' epigenetic memories are somehow capable of nudging even non-practitioners in certain directions? It has already been shown that metabolic changes, and experiences of trauma can have generations of impact on a family.[7] We've also seen that participants with the most Elder Folk DNA continue to this day to express small skull shape and alterations and even brain shape differences, ones similar to that species.[8] If epigenetic memories cross generations and brain shape changes are pronounced could there be some way in which ordinary people can sense things about these minority ancestors they shouldn't be able to?

If time can't necessarily stop such an influence, because we are indeed our ancestors walking, we could see those supposedly extinct forebears as having a continued life in our animal senses and their form of primal knowing, which in my practice we call the fetch. If this is so there is there a reason that certain people might not get ridden, even by some of our oldest ancestors, even the ones that weren't Sapiens? Could there be some poetic connection that links the ND characteristics in someone like Gooch, with his obsession with the ultimate of outsider-insiders who gave their actual face to the stereotypical witch? The Elder Folk?

We could begin with earlier theories about a relationship between ND people and our Elder Folk heritage. Perhaps even more suggestively we could bring up the way some of the genes modern humans inherited from the Denisovans sits adjacently to DNA associated with those exhibited in autism. Within these connections we might have found enough material to construct an academic-sounding language to explain why I choose to link this topic with the others we've touched on. However, if we are interested in the applicability of this material to using the story-structure of something visceral and luna-leaning as witchcraft, we must choose to explore this idea that sometimes some people in particular, people that in witchcraft might be described as carrying a Mark, have an inbuilt understanding of something ancient, with its roots in Other soil. We are made up of some very old, quite aware ancestors, still walking.

We have spoken earlier about the importance of stories on the way we treat other people. In some ways if we think we're too good to even play-act at a story because we're so reactive to it, to imagine pretending to believe it in the spirit of play, then we inherently view the people who think from the basis of that story as inferior to ourselves. In service of a willingness to pursue thinking through a number of stories, comparing them and otherwise respecting them with our attention we need to practice seeing scenarios through different story-lens. The witch's heightened ability, intrinsic and also developed via practice, to do this potentially makes our way of thinking far more imaginatively sophisticated than it has ever been understood or declared to be.

One place to start is to stop thinking about ND as real and somehow discovered at a certain point in history, and start thinking of it as the most recent story of how we explain a variety of forms of difference. In the past the ND individual would have simply been another Person of the Outside and if born in the wrong place at the wrong time, persecuted. If we perform this kind of gaze, this deviant gaze capable of changing its shape, on a regular enough basis we may become a little more flexible in terms of considering terms like Marked, as have been adopted and used in many witchcraft-practicing circles, or even the changeling faerie child, than we were before.

It should be added that ND people are nothing if not different to NT people and even more so to other ND people! Many do not like to be equated with not being human, being faeries, being People of the Outside, being witches, being descended from Elder Folk. Others find some kind of identification with the storybook Other that allows them to explain their experience to be powerful. I would go so far as to say that the code-breakers and mathematicians often fall into the first category and the musicians and artists into the latter. Those who do not obviously possess a recognised, monetarily salient savant skill are likely to be more unpredictable. The point being, like any large group, there is a variety of perspectives possible and it forms an errant judgment to reduce all of the members to sharing one viewpoint, or operating through one story-of-ourselves. Being able to story switch is in a way is more effective in achieving understanding, and basically it's also more polite.

This appreciation, rather than just tolerance, for diversity leads us to consider whether we want to experience all parts of the brain rather than only dignifying the firing of our pre-frontal cortex? If we do we might consider the use of different stories for different contexts or audiences. At our best moments we can code-switch back and forth with conscious awareness that we are doing so, we can announce that we're doing it, and our savvy listeners or readers will understand what is happening. They will be able to switch on over with us. What this amounts to is a different way of understanding truth, that something can be true in different ways, in different environments, or contexts. This is not just an idea but a practice.

Here is an example: if you are just looking after your health then herbs are probably better for you than most pharmaceuticals. But if you're in the middle of an emergency life and death scenario certain things like radiation, things very close to being poisons, may be needed to cheat death. In this way we don't need to become loving of one option and hating of the other, we only need to be flexible to circumstance. If we can teach our Sapien brains this technique there is no reason things need become faith-based, where people come to be dedicated to only 'natural' approaches to their health.

Such code-switching won't happen in most environments because you'd almost say that the over-culture is designed to avoid this kind of thinking and to set up the conditions for war. This is probably because of strong black-serpent power, a reactiveness to danger, outsiders, and fearfulness. Some people who practice spirituality or religion are already thinking like this if they accept that science has a place in their world in certain situations. When this kind of thinking does blossom we are gifted with a certain felicity of association that may allow room to open up, room to open up in the new disruption we've caused, thus making-reality more textured than some of us are relaxed enough to accept. The disruption itself holds the key to the gift.

Of course, such a thing requires us to become very emotionally observant, very mentally flexible, and less exclusion driven. I would argue that these are not some of Sapiens' original strong points — or maybe it appears like this because of generations of the epigenetic memory of trauma... My grandfather flew planes in World War II, my great grandfather flew planes in World War I and lost many comrades. One can assume that my grandmothers were at home dealing with rations, stress and the fear of invasion. Some families have three generations of war, with parents that endured Vietnam added to this list. It would make sense if this recent violent history had left the marks of exclusive nationalism on some families, as sad as the results of this can often be.

Here is another example of another way of approaching things: as someone who once considered themselves an academic in training I would talk about Others, and various occulted subgroups and occasionally ND as a neurological-exile category. As a writer on the subject of a deed without a name I might then also talk about Marked people, changeling-like phenomenon, or faerie descent as ways to recognise a Person of the Outside. This isn't just two different vocabularies this is two entirely different ways of seeing the world, both of them applicable to certain circumstances. Those who are fascinated by the idea of singularity, binaries, war between binary oppositions, and arid consistency might see this as a flaw in my thinking, but in my experience it has been one of my strongest muscles, allowing me to pass information between the two and form a three.

It might seem pedantic to point this out during this chapter on ND, yet it seems oddly fitting given the tendency for ND people to be pedantic. Later we will see how this ability to multi-story, to work more than one story cognitively and emotionally, without necessarily giving sole dominance to only one, is precisely the skill we need to fully understand witchcraft, and its links to our hybridity. Even from an intellectual angle alone it is truly worth trying to understand. Because something threatening, by a variety of different names throughout the world, has existed in cultures so far apart in distance and likely shared origin that it's remarkable how obsessed Sapiens are with this topic. One could put it down to paranoia, or the need to have an excuse to scapegoat the strange person, yet the shared details between these cultural stories are truly remarkable.

Pretending in a book like this to subscribe to the story of reason alone would be to provide a fake bifurcation. It would be to pretend that we know a lot about things we are still exploring, such as epigenetic memory and its potential power. Whereas to work away at spinning ideas from at least two very different story-spools can only get us closer to what we might come to term: a witchcraft brain-heart-gut logic, one that gives equal weighting to all parts of the thinking body. Sometimes to really understand something you have to come close to thinking like it, and like Shreeve tried to do for Neanderthals, feeling like it. Behind the story of reason there is a truth a lot more potent, that something in me already knew about this connection between witches and some very ancient human history, something inhuman, something we can't outrightly prove a connection to, but can definitely sense. This is something that one might call an intuitive knowing, which whilst it doesn't explain the practical formation of witchcraft during the persecutions in Europe, for instance, it certainly presses close to the fact a related idea of the predatory sorcerer who cannot help her night-flights is very common around the world for Sapiens.

It is a story shaped much like a labyrinth rather than a straight line, it is the widdershins part of the spider's web that is laid down first and eaten later in the creation process, whereas rationality provides the uprights and the clockwise spiral that comes afterwards. It comes from a type of knowing that is perhaps more a thing of the blood and guts and marrow, the red knowledge of the fetch intelligence in the body. Of course, in the world of words that inevitably derive from our ego, our aggressive, acquisitive gaze, it is more of a question than an answer. Which is perhaps part of its Virtue.

The question is important because it relates to all of our human experience, and maybe touches the edges of why minority groups, who may be cognitively, sexually, or otherwise different, all belong to once related categories. We find here traces of alien thinking or what we might prefer to term, the returned gaze of the People of the Outside, the deviant gaze, as we choose to talk back.

Before we go any further I'd like to bring up an example of ancient myth-making which impresses us with the fact that long term stories hold, stories that might go all the way back to when Sapiens was still a single group. The prohibition against pointing at a rainbow is found throughout South-East Asia, India, North America, among the Atsugewi of northern California and the Lakota of the northern plains; in remote parts of Australia, and isolated islands in Melanesia; among the Nyabwa of Ivory Coast and the Kaiwá of Brazil. The Grimms brothers also noted it was present in Germany. It is found in one hundred and twenty four cultures worldwide.[9]

The prohibition is so similar, often involving some unpleasant penalty for your finger, that it is suggested to have been a very early Sapien belief, one that has survived for all this time over great distances and many eras. The fact that Australia is included in this list makes the likelihood of a viral dissemination happening later in history extremely unlikely, as Aboriginal cultures are at least fifty-thousand years old and more likely over seventy-thousand years old. In essence the rainbow is considered a manifestation of a holy or Otherworldly location, or a glimpse of the serpent of creation itself, and pointing is usually considered rude, as it's an aggressive form of the gaze. Even with this prohibition remaining the same across the world we can see that truly ancient cultural memory, both of Ice Ages and rainbows, are indeed possible.

What this tells us is that when dealing with some of the modern manifestations of difference — whether they be people's concerns over LGBTQ people's existence, women's bodies in general, or neurodivergence, we can see that some of our reactiveness as a species can reach back a long way in history. Prohibition is very impactful for Sapiens and tends to remain intact, especially if some form of shame of punishment (such as being made to thrust the offending finger into buffalo dung as with the rainbow pointing taboo) is attached to making that cultural mistake. Given that we see rainbow serpents in both Australia and African Vodou as Ayida-Weddo it seems this might point to the memory of a very ancient god-form.

When I was a teenager I realise looking back that I tended to make friends with a lot of other ND people. The friendships or relationships that never went anywhere usually consisted of attempting to connected with NT people. As they say when it comes to autism if you've met one person with autism, you've met one person with autism. So it is trying to say the least to reduce the meaning behind such a diagnosis down to key things that must be there what we do find is evidence of a different structuring pattern to the individual's whole fabric of reality, one that is so pervasive its almost difficult to explain.

In other words ND people, whether declared boy or girl at birth, all seem to have one thing that a plethora of their other characteristics hinge on, the fact they believe social reality to work a certain way, a way that doesn't line up with how it works for NT people. This is to suggest that the squeaky hinge that many people associated with ND might not in fact act out against the social wants of NT people, (and perhaps it is a good idea to get away from letting NT people define what is wrong with an autistic people at all?) it may in fact have a lot more to do with how reality is processed. My daughter is diagnosed with autism and one of the major issues that she had as a child was a kind of invisibility belief about herself. It was strong enough that she failed to understand that you can't just do something which isn't socially acceptable in a semi-public or entirely public space. and imagine that people won't watch you and judge you. You are always the subject of an aggressive gaze. It sounds very simple when you word it like that, and probably linked to the widely preferred lack of eye contact. When you unpack this notion it seems to all hang on a kind of thinking that isn't based around such plethora of social judgment. It took her a long time to realise that other people were constantly judging each other via their gaze.

It was not so much that she thought she was invisible, more that her mind was tired with keeping up with the social rules of the group and she would run out of the ability to mask and forget others were watching her. This could be seen as a kind of delusion or failing or as the term Autism Spectrum Disorder names it, a kind of disorder. As a perspective that falls down when you cease to take the typical cognitive pattern as the place from which you judge things. I would argue there is good reason to consider doing this, as such behaviours make things difficult in the world for the ND individual there are also a lot of gains to be imagined. For instance, a great deal of social awkwardness in ND people derives from shame responses to the amount of times they've been pointed out as different or ostracised.

For some ND people it's possible to bend this differing perspective in directions that makes some quite successful in late capitalism — which, of course, is dreadfully important to most people's thriving. As long as their masking is better than, say, Mozart's, they usually are allowed some space to be different as long as the end product is considered worth something. Sadly this takes us a long way from the tribal cultures where diverse people were considered sacred. It is worth paying attention to the fact that cursed and sacred are two stories that we tell about people who are different, both with very different outcomes. As we should know many lower functioning ND people were killed during the Third Reich.

Although I haven't been able to spare the time or money for adult diagnosis for myself I am fairly sure that my daughter inherits her ND nature from me, and understanding this has enabled me to better make use of the abilities that for myself come with ND. For some ND folk that direction for success could be coding, or it could be music, there are many highly focused individuals that have used their One Very Important Topic to become renowned marine biologists.

Sometimes that gift has a connection between being able to step back from aspects of the group mind (paradigms) to stack reality-matrix' or perhaps play with more than one at once.

If we take a step back from what others just assume as the backdrop to reality because to them it is familiar and therefore invisible, and stop making all their decisions in relation to it, they will notice a few things about ourselves as a primarily Sapien person. One would be that our ability to think about certain groups of other people is actually quite limited by comparison to our other forms of intelligence. Most people seem motivated by things as simple as catch phrases, maybe even ones we learned from movies or TV. Whilst at this stage science hasn't allowed us to fully explore what the larger cerebellum of the Neanderthal human might have made possible,[10] at the same time we have no way of knowing if these limitations with understanding other groups was common to them also. We certainly know they preferred to live in smaller groups than we do. This is a characteristic they share with both the witch and the ND individual, who are usually known either for cottages on the edge of the woods, for struggling with the effort to maintain large numbers of friendships, or worse still, catastrophically failing to maintain the positive regard of their community.

Whilst we don't see that as a sign of success in the over-culture these seeming-limitations are not necessarily a negative. The tendency of Sapiens to group together and bother themselves constantly about what other people are up to, gossip about what they think those people are thinking and what they're doing with whom, is part of the fodder for great deal of wars, bigotry, hate crimes, and violent prejudice, aimed at races, genders, and sexual preferences. Giving each other a little space, both physically and in regards to our obsession with projecting our opinions over others life-styles would get rid of a lot of the material levelled at so called infidels, libertines, breakers of 'natural law', and non-believers.

It could be seen as hubristic to assume that the social patterns of ND people, witches, and even our ancient cousins they are somehow a disorder by comparison to Sapien habits. The idea that these cousins of our shared heritage all shared our common Sapien weaknesses with us is another form of hubris, added to by the assumption they also lacked our strengths... That sounds to me like a green screen we've created based on our own emotional attachment to ourselves as a species, one against which we hope to project a positive image of ourselves. Something that is hardly surprising considering that whilst many of us have been championing reason for some time we have remained very blind to the way that the emotions of the normative and the powerful amongst us drive most of our collective decisions.

This leads us to the important point that there are many types of intelligence, beyond the type that Sapiens are famous for. There is emotional intelligence, something with which I would argue our own current species is probably quite challenged. The mini brains that have been grown in the laboratory of the Neanderthal brain inform us that their skulls held something quite different to our own. We can infer that they were capable of seeing in lower light and probably for a longer distance, as far as practical things go. Though nobody seems to have been able to answer questions about what that would mean to their full cognition at a psychological level. Perhaps darkness was less frightening to them — to begin with? How would that impact their religious life? What if our assumption that light is good and darkness is bad is purely a Sapien point of view?

Whether or not their emotional intelligence was higher than ours is a mystery, though it doesn't seem unlikely to suggest it could have been so, given their extended need to survive glacial conditions in close contact with one another for warmth and sustenance. Sapiens have a smaller cerebellum than Neanderthals, which likely changes our experience of our bodies and senses, but maybe also our emotional understanding, dream-life, ability to dream share, dealing with and maybe even intuiting unwordable emotional realities, and perhaps even the existence of nuances between binaries. It might even, as Shreeve's writing expressed, mean that our connection between our own bodies and those of other Sapiens is less developed as an extra sense than it was among the Elder Folk.

We like to imagine that all virtues of consciousness are unique to our own species, yet we don't think too much about the fact that our current humanity is derived from a variety of genetic material and that all our strengths may not have arisen from original Sapiens. It is quite possible that some things we view as virtues might also derive not from the Cro-Magnon heritage we possess and therefore from some of the other contributors as well. There are now even some suggestions being put forward that our Elder People were the first artists to paint caves in ochre[11] and certainly seem to have preceded Sapien use of red ochre hand-prints in art and ritual.

I am about to code switch a little. To take a step back from the discussion and think about its meaning in a different context.

Let us take an excursion to the two major roads of Righteousness and Sin that are described in the story of Thomas the Rhymer, of Scottish extract, and his abduction into Elphame, meaning Elf-home. This holy location is a place which he can only reach through walking up to the knee along a path thoroughly awash with red blood, taking us back to the importance of the colour red and Sapien avoidance of pathways lathed in blood. These two roads are the two major binaries via which Sapien religions seem to think everything works. This is illustrated by the fact that large tracts of our world are covered in humans who believe things are good or bad, white or black, male or female, blessed or damned, self or other. Generally speaking the rules are kept nice and simple so as to be understood by all and breaking them attracts punishment.

The idea that others in the group, not even in our own group necessarily, might be, or be living, differently to one's self in some other way, even if it's in private, has been a source of major concern for Sapiens throughout history. This seemingly dysfunctional tendency has demonstrated our lack of functionality by leading to witch hunts, it has led to racial purges, it has led to Reichs and persecution of people with diseases. What this history of hatred for difference points to is that our obsession with binaries and conformity and difficulty dealing with things that are neither one thing nor the other has been a major source of loss of human life and the inspiration for some terrible cruelties.

One example of the general distrust felt even in some gay-accepting communities towards bisexuality and transgender people, particularly when this quality arises among men. Often being bisexual is read as a code for the person being on the road to announcing they are gay. Few forms of discrimination cut across both the straight and LGBTQ community the way this one does. This kind of thinking represents one of our most dangerous traits as a species. We struggle with third options, you are either with something, or you are against it. If you are with it you need to talk a certain way so that everyone can tell you are that way from your speech and your physical gestures. If there is a third way, a crooked misty grey path between these two black and white ones, to take another code-shift back into witchcraft terminology, then most people don't understand it or accept it, basically because they assume it means you have a choice.

Whilst limited studies on human sexuality announced, but later disproved, that bisexual men (despite their best protestations!) do not exist,[12] numerous men continue to identify themselves as bisexual and have sex with more than one sex. Later studies have admitted that bisexual men do in fact exist. Whether it is accepted or not this third more crooked and interesting path is essential to people being able to get along, as it provides a sense there is indeed, as Kinsey suggested, a sliding scale when it comes to sexuality. There must be somewhere to rest that is neither a vehement hatred for something or total embrace of it. We need stories that utilise the magic of both up and down, and all the paths between them, one that not only recognises male and female, but the many crossroads of different degrees of the characteristics we call masculine and feminine, that help to form creative interaction between them. If there is such a story-web available then we very much need to find it and make use of it before we kill or threaten any more human beings.

If, as we have learned about ourselves, we are indeed made up of the genetic material of at least two different species, is there not at least a triple-ness to our nature, a biological Otherness available to our imagination? This triplicity could very well be the medicine our world age requires more than anything. This idea of a third way, one that relates to the third road to Elphame, that blood-reddened track that so many Sapien cultures have tabooed, one that might also have appealed to other human species, could it be the one that might even lead to the diversity of desires and ways of thinking to be found repressed in current-day Sapiens? Although at this stage it can't be proved it would be remarkable if we, as the place these ancestors' species went to die/live-on, had not left some mark on us psychologically, as well as on our skull and brain shape?

It is extraordinary to be the first generations of Sapiens to begin thinking of ourselves not as the final end of evolution, where all intelligence came to some sort of peak, but a hybrid-vigourous creature that can draw on all sides of our nature, rather than just one out of two binaries. We now know ourselves as something made up of a few different possible ways of being, a few different mixed natures, there is room for multiple stories and the complexity of that, of different stories being true in different ways...

Whilst this kind of thinking might sound like a strain at first, for many it is a lot like getting the body stronger by going to the gym. If you expose yourself more often to things that surprise and unsettle you it will help you to remain supple. It does something to the spirit just living through this moment in history. This third-path can be experiential, it can be play, it doesn't have to be only available to witches or academics. We can model it in storytelling, art, and even in the way we speak about people. It's really not necessarily scary to change the way we talk about others.

ND is by far not a primitive trait, if anything its part of the hyper-variable monstrosity that gave way to much of our brilliance, and also much of the dangers that founded our brilliance. Nor do I intend to make a direct parallel between ND and changeling status which are very different stories, or to attribute species hybridity of any unusual amount to ND people. All of these stories could be held in one brain, one brain which is never alone, it is part of a network of other consciousnesses who are working away at these mysteries, shining up different corners of the genie-bottle. The ND brain emerges from a place in our genetic tininess where humanity is holding its Wild Cards, and some of that genetic creativity has come from a wider more diverse genetic profile gifted to us by an array of Sapiens and Others.

Although there are no final answers yet about the origins of autism what genetic evidence we do have suggests that ND would not have existed amongst Neanderthals or Denisovans. The genes associated with it are found in a highly unstable, pro-mutation part of our genome, what is called a hyper-variable zone. It might even be proven in the future that ND is one of the results of a variation that is a combination of Sapien genes with Neanderthal and Denisovan genes, rather than something that existed in any of those three older populations. Perhaps the feeling of growth in this population is due to ND people finding each other more easily in this era more ND children are being diagnosed than before?

If the Elder Folk didn't just disappear or go extinct as we've been inclined to say up until recently, and instead were woven into us, then perhaps that potential for genetic diversity that Sapiens holds is their long term gift to us, who are also Them? Perhaps we haven't even fully gazed at the consequences of their contribution, as yet, and yet we're walking around manifesting it all the same. Maybe we are not the owners of the gaze that will do that Seeing, and those eyes are yet to open. Some part of us will survive into that future, the part of us that is Their ancestor of blood or spirit.

Those genetic hyper-variables where mutations most often occurs in the human genome are the source of many of our greatest leaps into complexity, as well as a lot of mysterious seeming idling whose purpose is more mysterious. To put it in the simplest terms, one might say that this little powerhouse of possibilities in our genes is where every rapid, major, evolutionary change in humans has come from. You could almost say that as a ND person, whilst no more directly linked to the pre-Sapien heritage than anyone else, you are part of the human genome's experimental category, where this hybrid gene structure has been trying out potentially useful extremes and differences.

If we could move from being a species intent on persecuting anyone who doesn't act, behave, and conform in the same manner as everyone else, we might just be able to grease up the crooked riding pole we've been handed and take to the skies.

Because witchcraft is probably the meta-narrative, much like the world-wide rainbow pointing prohibition, that remembers the parts of our own background that we feel uncomfortable with, in awe of, and often afraid of.

Notes

1. David Graeber and David Wengrow, *The Dawn of Everything: A New History of Humanity.*, Farrar, Straus and Giroux, (2021).

2. David Graeber and David Wengrow, *The Dawn of Everything.*, p. 97.

3. Ibid., p. 102.

4. Edward J. Hollox, Luciana W. Zuccherato, Genome Structural Variation in Human Evolution., Trends in Genetics, (2021) https://doi.org/10.1016/j.tig.2021.06.015

5. G. Pfuhl, & L. Ekblad, Neurodiversity traits linked to Neanderthal Admixture. (2018) https://doi.org/10.31219/osf.io/w4nh5

6. Edward J. Hollox, Luciana W. Zuccherato, op cit.

7. Anne Brunet. Bridging The Transgenerational Gap With Epigenetic Memory. Trends In Genetics, vol 29, no. 3, 2013, pp. 176-186. Elsevier BV, doi:10.1016/j.tig.2012.12.008 Accessed 19 Nov 2022.

8. Gregory MD, et al, Neanderthal-Derived Genetic Variation Shapes Modern Human Cranium and Brain. Sci Rep. 2017 Jul 24;7(1):6308. doi: 10.1038/s41598-017-06587-0. PMID: 28740249; PMCID: PMC5524936.

9. Robert Blust, Pointing, Rainbows, and the Archaeology of Mind., Anthropos. 116. (2021) pp.145-162. 10.5771/0257-9774-2021-1-145.

10. Though there are currently very small Neanderthal brains being grown to try to understand how they differ from our own, and the spoiler is that they look very different.

11. Emma Marris, Neanderthal Artists Made Oldest-Known Cave Paintings., Nature, (2018), https://www.nature.com/articles/d41586-018-02357-8 Accessed 19 Nov 2022.

12. Dr Gerulf Rieger's study in 2005 apparently disproved that male bisexuality exists at all but he later discovered that it clearly did and published a U-turn admitting it does exist. Sadly the authors of *Sex Before Dawn* cited the original study declaring that women were attracted to 'everything' and that men in general were either gay or straight.

Chapter 9

They All Lived Together in a Crooked Little House

As we have said, the Sapien mind seems to have a great interest in the number two. The over-culture we are a part of loves binaries and might have religions with Holy Trinities but fundamentally we see only two genders and we get dreadfully upset when someone says this isn't the case.[1] There are a motley crew of people very committed to the idea of two genders, people who would deem themselves feminists, and also men's rights activists who feel terribly under threat from this different way of being. What we've learned about epigenetic memory makes it likely this behaviour is a result of intergenerational trauma, the type that activates the black-serpent in our bodies over many lifetimes in a family line. This intergenerational trauma can make some people's behaviour seem inexplicable.

This is worthy of notice because when people are deeply committed to something as abstract as asserting that everyone else also believe there is nothing in between the concept of Two, well, those people usually have something to gain from the binary. People who are biologically afraid, as in having a physical threat response, are usually seeking to gain something for themselves and other people like themselves, even if they aren't conscious of it. Or at least they believe they will gain something... When you think about it the number two is more often used as a method of control and even to situate the conditions of warfare. If you're not with us, you're against us. There is our side, and there is the enemy side.

Due to this black serpent way of thinking things are all too often viewed as either benefiting men, or benefiting women, benefiting those born in a country, or benefiting immigrants.

Apparently you can only look after veterans in your own country by ignoring another category and veterans will be thrown at you if you err in this. The truth is, however, there are a variety of people who do not need to be classed as enemies that we are still very vexed by because part of us feels they pose some sort of threat to the vision of the world we grew up with or that they are competitors for resources. There are hints carried along by the winds of change that a large part of humanity finds this idea quite limiting and is tired of this mindset of struggle, with their own quality of life being the object of that struggle. I'm not referring entirely to LGBTQ identification, but to something far stranger and stronger that I sense to be afoot. The idea that it is impossible to benefit one of the two gender groups made available, without benefiting both, without the situation leading to a condition based on force or oppression.

Treating humanity as if we were two separate interest groups ignores the fact that one of these so-called groups must give birth to, and in many cultures, raise both of the other genders. The two must also fraternise to some extent for the creation of new life. Trying to treat the two as having their own individual interests that do not cross-fertilise means we ask Sapien people to cut off half of their empathic experience for their species. When this happens in other animals you end up with a Chimpanzee existence instead of a Bonobo one, or a domestic Orangutang experience like the murder story of Doe by Sugito. But there is also this tantalising sensation that we might be able to some extent choose, through exercise and awareness, which way we see and behave. The idea that the genders even come from different planets like Mars and Venus is absurd. It runs up close to racism when considering which idea of Sapiens is really the most stupid. We are, after all, one species, so the idea that pigmentation of the skin is taken to denote rank or value is beyond absurd and based on the desire to take things off another group. The idea of a war of types, between the actual sexes of our species shows something quite diseased about the individualism of the over-culture. We aren't men and women at all, not in a deeper sense, we are all invested members of the Sapien species.

As Sapiens we are not a unit of self that operates against all other selves, as is clear when observing our methods for survival and our current struggles termed 'environmental'. This is best illustrated by the way that campaigns to get men to sympathise with the problem of sexual abuse of women often take the approach of reminding men that each woman is someone's 'sister or mother'. Sometimes this is answered by crossing out sister or mother and so that the slogan merely reads: she is someone. It takes some true mental gymnastics (or religious ones) to explain how a second sex of greater value comes forth from one who is lesser, and even why we feel the need to decide which part of our species is greater and lesser.

In the bulk of human cultures there is some sort of explanation for the different status given to the sexes, though most of them are not more persuasive to me than the simple fact we are clearly part of a continuum of life with all other hominids, and beyond that with all of life itself. If we fail to recognise this egalitarianism of life-value in time we will destroy our lifestyle, and the lives of many human and non-human beings in the process. We must always ask ourselves who stands to benefit from a story we tell, and who is to fall victim to it. The very fact that this is something that needs pointing out at all exposes us to one of Sapiens' greatest failings — lack of emotional intelligence. Or perhaps, more correctly, difficulty processing trauma in a manner that uplifts rather than oppresses others.

By processing I don't just mean having empathy with others, I mean the kind of social commonsense that allows. For instance, for us to acknowledge the relaxed happiness of the men of Mosuo in China, where a sex-positive, female empowered lifestyle reigns and there is no shaming around sexual expression regardless of gender. The traditions of the Mosuo[2] are often interpreted as a matriarchy when they look to me instead merely like the absence of a violent patriarchy, and what even might amount to the surprisingly easy business of egalitarian living. As we have lived so long in a state of struggle with one another it is hard for us to conceive of the idea that not everyone in our own household is necessarily our competitor. Generations of living like this has likely also riddled their population with the black serpent impulses to possess and over-power.

One only needs to consider the way male-on-male violence is used to squash the huge differences and variation that naturally emerge in the behaviour of an entire half of the species. The place of violence as a method of forcing away certain attitudes is clear the moment we consider how much more difficult people find it to reason and to develop their intellect when they are subjected to threat and violence from an early age.[3] What is missing when we as a species are subjected to regular violence isn't just the ability to discuss emotions, but the ability to process and flush them out in productive ways, through ritual or play.

Despite the many attempts, (usually but not always done by the people of the gender that stands to benefit most from keeping the line nice and well-drawn) to strenuously segregate the genders into well-marked boxes, it is clearly at least partially a forlorn hope. Queer people who break both sexuality and gender norms seem to continue to exist, especially in cultures where penalties have fallen away, and revealingly even in cultures where the penalty is still death. The inherent disobedience of human desire for self-expression, for pleasure, for connection with other humans at these key positions is that vital to people in cultures all around the world. Unless you belong to a worldview that treats you like a child, probably due to its own difficult history, and places all the emphasis on conformity and punishment it must be clear that something emerging all around the world, even under threat of death is clearly part of our human diversity. We don't even need to understand why Grandmother Nature deemed people to be sexually aroused by a variety of things, we only need to accept that she knows what she's doing. Her major calling card seems to be variety.

It's easy to think that we get a choice of some kind as a Sapien person, whether we want to see ourselves as connected more with the more violent and oppressive life of Chimpanzee or the sex-positive life of the Bonobo. Whether or not it is as simple as a choice is another matter. It's likely it would take some time for people to outgrow impulses coming from the black serpent response. Amongst Chimpanzees the weaker members are dominated and not allowed to have access to meat foods unless the dominant males who killed the animal say so, violence is a regular solution to disagreement. In the other group grooming and sex is used to calm down inter-group tensions and usually results in a good response from the troop. Groups of females who are sexually active with each other are able to defend themselves if necessary because of their solidarity.[4]

It's arguable that these two groups of Chimpanzee-affiliated apes are more different to each other than any so-called races alive today. This may indicate the level of difference that might exist between our own Sapien perspective, different as they are between cultures, and those of the Elder Folk. Genetically the difference between our species and Chimpanzees and Bonobos is about the same, so it would be easy to come to the conclusion that they represent two polarities of our nature. This would also be due to Sapien tendency to see everything as reflecting on us, as we are clearly the centre of the universe... Despite this genetic fact there are also a number of things that biologically link Sapiens more to the Bonobo. For instance Bonobo chimpanzees find being on their back legs more comfortable than Chimpanzees do, they possess a finger length ratio that is closer to that of the Sapien hand,[5] and a forward facing vulva in the manner of a Sapien that causes the females to prefer forward facing sex. The ovulation of a Bonobo is not telegraphed like it is in other apes, so Bonobo females have sex throughout their cycle with some small variations, just as Sapiens do.

Whilst there is no patrolling of fatherhood amongst Bonobos, or male control of female sexual activities, there is a great deal of bisexual encounters in both sexes.[6] This is interesting considering how many of our own species feel about the liminal zone of bisexuality, especially male bisexuality. It can be hard for people who were raised to fear violence from their fellows to get their heads around how such a species manages to thrive. Nonetheless, it's clear that Bonobos have a method of using sex to diffuse aggression or hostility and create non-biological bonds between females that allow their power to equal that of the males.

This doesn't mean they are fur angels by pro-LGBTQ, sex positive Sapien ethical standards, as they regularly include prepubescent Bonobos in their sexual activities, who seem quite involved, and they also engage in certain forms of incest.[7] Naturally it isn't necessary for other species to be fur angels by our standards. There are some exceptions, such as children raised by the mother together, but by and large incest is not a taboo for them to the degree it is for most Sapiens. Whilst this behaviour is probably some distance from that of the Elder Folk it may be a more extreme version of their practices, and our own colourful fantasies we might play with but would never want to put into practice could also fall somewhere on this spectrum of using sex for co-regulation.

It's noteworthy that there are also a variety of Sapien indigenous cultures[8] that manage to find a role and purpose for queer (bisexual and transgender specifically) behaviour without losing out on babies. Given that these cultures are from the same species as us and this degree of difference is possible between us, and say, certain other Sapien cultures who currently meet homosexuality with a hangman's noose, it is clear that attitudes of this sort can be quite various even among Sapiens. I would guess these differences have to do with the amount of danger those cultures have witnessed and how hardwired they have become to view the world in terms of us and them, good and bad, survival or death.

The difference between the Bonobo and the Chimpanzee is even larger than the difference between not what Sapiens claim to do sexually, and what Sapiens actually do sexually in private, or play at doing. What we fantasise about, what we watch porn about, what we do without telling anyone else, is far closer to the Bonobo than it is to the Chimpanzee, or they to one another. This disparity between what we claim we do in an over-culture and what we actually do in private suggests a fairly large schism in our psyche that I believe must be explained and hopefully eventually, tended.

When it comes to competition for mates and sexual violence we Sapiens have this in our history and in our present world. But all the way back to the Professor Kinsey's report on sexuality it is possible to see that this doesn't even come close to defining what we are really doing when we're alone. Whilst its easiest to see the worst of Sapien behaviour in Chimpanzee-language, where female consent is optional, there just isn't as much evidence of a physical connection between Chimpanzees and Sapiens when it comes to their sexual and reproductive body as there is between Bonobos and ourselves.

You will notice that I have chosen not to treat these primate third-cousins of ours as if they were somehow less relevant groups. I've done this on purpose because I think if we're going to cut loose from some of the intellectually binding, binary, and frankly somewhat simplistic notions that suffocate the worldview of many Sapiens, then we are going to have to get past the idea that there is some fundamental difference between ourselves and other primates. Witches have always had a closer connection with other animals due to our tendency to transform into them, and to sup on their unique dreaming life.

It might seem demeaning to say that because Bonobos and Chimpanzees look quite similar to each other but are so different in their mating and violence behaviour that we can't guess much about the differences between Sapiens and the Elder Folk. That if that difference can exist between these two other hominids then perhaps radically different ways of being human were experienced by our lesser represented ancestors like Neanderthals and Denisovans? And how might this repressed aspect of our humanity have fed into the forbidden core of thoughts and deeds deemed to be witchcraft? How might this projection have fed into the deviant acts that witches are accused of all around the world?

Outside of witchcraft many are so used to the idea that the dark is morally inferior to the light, yet we come to this conclusion based on our own physiological limits. As Sapiens do not see very well in low light we were naturally afraid of mega-faunal animals emerging from it right from the beginning. What if instead of a moral value we are simply not capable of seeing as well as the Neanderthals probably were? What if Seasonal Affective Disorder in our own population was a hangover from Neanderthal DNA where they developed a semi-hibernation mode to cope with intense glacial winters? What if winter wasn't meant to be more miserable than summer? There is also the matter of voice pitch. In Sapien cultures a lower voice pitch is associated with masculinity and a deeper voice is usually considered authoritative. This whole way of thinking might have to be imagined away when dealing with Neanderthals. Due to the shape of the vocal tract, experts on voice theorise that the male Neanderthal voice was much higher than the male Sapien voice.[9] How would this have impacted notions of gender among their species?[10] We should also keep in mind the fact that they made musical instruments that match the notes of the

Do, Re, Mi scale, allowing us to assume they possessed musical instincts.[11]Whilst these points open us mainly to speculation they show us ways in which small physiological differences could change our experience of our world in radical ways.

Another thing we know about the breeding habits of the Neanderthal people is that usually a cave or other settlement was inhabited by brothers.[12] The women who joined them there were genetically more various. I have heard speculation that this suggested either that the society of the Elder Folk (whatever 'society' actually meant when we could actually be looking at a series of groups or nations with differing practices is another question) was patriarchal-leaning. This suggestion is an odd one, because this is another practice that the Elder Folk seem to share with Bonobos, who are generally considered to be egalitarian. It's almost as if there is something in even the smartest Sapien scholar that wants to find Neanderthals to be inferior and worthy of their own extinction in favour of us.

Sapiens are excellent at gathering information, yet as soon as we have it we tend to shape it to please the black serpent, to feed into our own current political position, allegiances, fears, or insecurities. Sometimes it happens in an even worse way where we end up feeding assumptions that we carry about our own place in the cosmos that we're entirely innocent of possessing. What we do know is that British culture, and pretty much all of the other cultures reaching back thousands of years before it, and around it in Europe, and even some places not particularly close to it, have been very interested in a two-by-two world of gender relations with men more or less leading, for a very long time. When it comes to piloting a world based on coercion it seems to be a powerful model.

From a European perspective we may ask if this obsession with things coming in twos and female oppression might only reach back to the Kurgan settling of Europe as Maria Gimbutas suggested, an event that has now been backed up with genetics?

We know a great deal of new genetic material entered Europe at this time, most of it in the form of Y (male) chromosomes.[13] Perhaps what Gimbutas calls Old Europe was in fact closer to egalitarian with a stronger emphasis on foremothers as she originally asserted? Instead of looking for Queendoms to answer all the Kingdoms, could there rather be a third way that eschews one part of the species being better than the other half? A way of thinking, or maybe a way of feeling, that allows us to indeed be one species with a common interest?

Something about witchcraft and its sixth awkward finger gets in the way of those two-by-two visions, where one might have expected a Kingdom, or even a Queendom, one finds themselves inside a Queerdom, something more crooked and surprising. Not because of the sexuality of witches, which is often diverse simply because aberrant gender is another of the many things that has been associated with witchcraft, but because witches have never been seen as anything other than aberrant. Even in Macbeth we hear the three witches or Fates described thus: 'you should be women but your beards forbid me to interpret you as such.'

Even today in some remote Aboriginal communities I have visited in the north of the continent the beard growth of post-menopausal women is seen as an enhancement to their position in society, rather than a disfigurement. We also often see women who do not behave according to the standards set out for women in various cultures being accused of witchcraft. The same thing in reverse happened during the persecution of The Templars where we saw male homosexual behaviour being part of the list of deviancies. Claims of heresy, especially of the persecution sort, have often involved claims of almost indiscriminate sexual expression, much like the Bonobo.

The claims have also involved a list of things like incest, age discrepancy, and, of course, also same sex relations. What heretics were accused of, even as early as the persecution of

Christians in Rome, were basically that they were living the sexual life of Bonobo Chimpanzees. When Sapien groups gather together in large numbers, and sometimes even in smaller numbers, it becomes a matter of anxiety-management, of the placating of the ever vigilant black serpent, to police the lives of other Sapiens, including whether those other Sapiens are engaging in sexual activities that others disapprove of or find disgusting. This is prevalent enough that a highly active disgust reaction, a type of black serpent response, is highly linked to conservative thinking.[14]

This fact in itself is quite remarkable. In terms of witches casting spells you can begin to understand why this would be banned by societies that acknowledge the reality of magic as an unfair advantage. But when it comes to who other people are having consensual, adult, sexual relations with it becomes a bit more difficult to find a way to claim that person is impacting others. Nonetheless, today in the US I still occasionally hear of freak weather events being the result of God's rage at homosexual activity. Whilst it sounds outrageous to any kind of thinker who recognises the unlikelihood of such childish and petty behaviour from a god, you can see what these people are doing. They are trying to find amidst their fear of difference a justification for why they wish to interfere in the private lives of others.

The best explanation is fear, something that is naturally common amongst domesticated animals. To return to Chimpanzees and Bonobos one of the most obvious behavioural differences that can be studied is that your standard Chimpanzee responds with fear and anxiety to the sound of a foreign call from another of their species they don't recognise. The Bonobo on the other hand responds with excitement.[15] The first species sees the foreign individual as a sign of approaching combat, whereas the latter sees it as a new bonding opportunity. The process of evolution that led to this could be seen as the result of some experiences that happened to the root populations of their ancestors. Both might have been helpful adaptations to their survival in a niche situation.

We need to be wary of assuming we have some kind of neutral perspective to offer on this topic, as we are all driven by fear and the desire for our group to succeed. If we interrogate our own sense of innocence we can do better towards those who are different to us, without necessarily endangering ourselves. Doing this allows us to reap the rewards they may bring. the better utilise our own hybrid brains, and basically just avoid being genocidal. To do this it would help to understand that whatever aspects of our apparently extinct ancestors made their way down to us, when they were morphed into witchcraft mythology, this was something done through the violent gaze, projection, or seeing through a mirror darkly. This negative perception of witchcraft would not represent its true nature, it would represent our own view of the magical practices of those rejected ancestor-peoples, the ones who hold the reportedly tainted blood. In other words, some of the ethical flaws we see there, some of the predatory motives also, are coming from an aspect of our own souls, intentions, and the forgotten stories of our own violent root-history.

This observation could take us a bit further towards explaining the belief in the witch's malevolence. This de-humanised status as cannibal and not-fully human, night-hag, sexual deviant etc... all of this could be seen as a worldwide preoccupation with warfare, anxiety, and the idea that somehow, somewhere there is someone working away against us, using startling similar methods to one another. Or, it could relate instead to a kind of reverse paranoia, the kind that arises in the dominant group when it knows very well that the victimised culture has every reason to come after them and try to eat them. Possibly because we may have in fact once eaten them. Like the German law against cannibalising witches, revenge cannibalism should also be on the table. Most likely though, there is a third explanation that partakes of both of these options and a little something extra.

Similar patterns seem to emerge in people wherever persecution exists. Those who do the persecution usually invent the idea that those they are set against are in fact planning something against them. This pattern is Sapiens being explicit about the fear that lies behind our persecution manias. We hear about it with the early-Christians, and you can even see it with gay agenda fears that evangelicals possess today. As the Witch of Endor demonstrated, it is a powerful position being outside the law of the city. If you are busy trying to keep women, who constitute a decent 51% of humanity, in a lower social position it makes sense that they must be storied to possess certain negative assets, such as the evil eye or killer menstrual blood. It has to be something biological that you can say the whole sex shares, that way there can be no exceptions. Even if some women have had a full hysterectomy, women are still storied to be cyclic and unpredictable. These differences must be deemed unchangeable, otherwise how could you account for truly claiming that over half of the human race all possess the same characteristics?

The truth is there is dizzying variety in the human species, in every sex, and every race. Given this, one can almost understand why people would want to make things simpler with stereotypes, it is so much easier to do away with stereotypes than it is to do away with whole groups of other people. This is likely why the rise of awareness about transgender people has threatened many. People becoming aware of various intersex conditions has also taken many to the event-horizon of their willingness to understand difference. This is before you even imagine how similar people coped with the existence of other human-like species when they used to roam the world...If your species has passed through land or resource shortage or severe hunting stress, to be set against a particular other species for a very long time the things you most fear about them will become patterns in stories told of them.

Someone might have once told tales of how the Elder Folk came into their camp when they were asleep at night and creepily rearranged their items yet stole nothing. The stories themselves would likely have begun to take on certain recognisable features, that due to Sapiens larger group and trading network would have been shared so quickly that we probably developed a unified folk mythos about the Older People. Knowing the way many pinkish people think about brownish people — a tiny distinction of appearance — one can only imagine how this storytelling would have impacted a world with multiple species of human. We may have developed unified stories about a people that were in fact quite different from place to place. I say this because this is often the case today when you hear people make stereotypical statements about something as ludicrously broad as 'Asians'. As it does today, and maybe more so, this could have led to dehumanisation.

These forbidden features of the Elder Folk, facial features as well as colouring and behavioural traits, can be seen to move together throughout Sapien cultures, spaced so far away from each other that there is clearly some far older shared experience. Among Sapien cultures from South East Asia to Britain the witch has a particular appearance which is similar to our cousins, she is often, though not always, a she. Included in this category are men who have contact with the blood through birth, sex, or proximity, widows, post-menopausal women, transgender women, and cross-dressers. She has associations with the colour red, menstrual blood carries numerous taboos, men's vital nature may be stolen, her magic is left-handed, and moves counter-clockwise, is associated with thirteen, he or she is not fully human, may pass down their taint in the blood, and is capable of cannibalising power, tainting pathways, and babies, or hag-riding their victims in the night.

Notes

1. There are also writers like the Franciscan priest Richard Rohr, author of Falling Upwards, who celebrates dynamism rather than dualism and focus on the actual trinity and resists the violence of projection of rejected characteristics onto others.

2. The peaceful Mosuo lifestyle that treats sex as a natural part of life is explored in detail in *Sex Before Dawn*, by Christopher Ryan.

3. G H, Bower, H Sivers, Cognitive Impact of Traumatic Events., Development and Psychopathology vol. 10,4 (1998): pp.625-53. doi:10.1017/s0954579498001795

4. Zanna Clay, Female Bonobos Use Copulation Calls As Social Signals., Biology Letters. (2022),https://royalsocietypublishing.org/doi/abs/10.1098/rsbl.2010.1227 Accessed 19 Nov 2022.

5. Matthew McIntyre, et al. Bonobos Have A More Human-Like Second-To-Fourth Finger Length Ratio (2D:4D) Than Chimpanzees: A Hypothesized Indication Of Lower Prenatal Androgens., Journal Of Human Evolution, vol 56, no. 4, 2009, pp. 361-365. Elsevier BV, doi:10.1016/j.jhevol.2008.12.004 Accessed 19 Nov 2022.

6. H. Ihobe, Male-male relationships among wild bonobos (Pan paniscus) at Wamba, Republic of Zaire. Primates 33, pp.163–179 (1992). https://doi.org/10.1007/BF02382747

7. Usually with the exception of siblings being cared for at the same time by the same mother. Bonobo Sexuality., Reed.Edu, 2022, https://www.reed.edu/biology/courses/BIO342/2011_syllabus/2011_websites/subramanian_jaime/genesis.html Accessed 19 Nov 2022.

8. Take for instance the variety of genders, including two-spirit people to be found among some American Indigenous peoples.

9. Patsy Rosenberg's High-pitched voice theory – Neanderthal – BBC science, https://youtu.be/o589CAu73UM

10. There is, of course, some contention on this reconstruction, with some saying their voices would have been more 'sing-song' than ours, and others even claiming they should be deeper than our own. It seems likely, however, that their capacity for speech was equal to our own. Conde-Valverde, Mercedes et al. Neanderthals And Homo Sapiens Had Similar Auditory And Speech Capacities. Nature Ecology &Amp; Evolution, vol 5, no. 5, 2021, pp. 609-615. Springer Science And Business Media LLC, doi:10.1038/s41559-021-01391-6 Accessed 24 Nov 2022.

11. Turk, Matija et al. The Mousterian Musical Instrument From The Divje Babe I Cave (Slovenia): Arguments On The Material Evidence For Neanderthal Musical Behaviour., L'anthropologie, vol 122, no. 4, 2018, pp. 679-706. Elsevier BV, doi:10.1016/j.anthro.2018.10.001 Accessed 24 Nov 2022.

12. L. Skov, & S. Peyrégne, et al. Genetic insights into the social organization of Neanderthals., Nature 610, pp. 519–525 (2022). https://doi.org/10.1038/s41586-022-05283-y

13. Haak, Wolfgang et al, Massive Migration From The Steppe Is A Source For Indo-European Languages In Europe. Cold Spring Harbor Laboratory, (2015) doi:10.1101/013433 Accessed 19 Nov 2022.

14. Y. Inbar, et al, Disgust Sensitivity, Political Conservatism, and Voting., Social Psychological and Personality Science, 3(5), (2012) 537–544. https://doi.org/10.1177/1948550611429024

15. J. Tan, et al, Bonobos respond prosocially toward members of other groups., Sci Rep 7, 14733 (2017). https://doi.org/10.1038/s41598-017-15320-w

Chapter 10

Inside the Skull Labyrinth

One of the great mysteries of our Sapien history is the source of the mythos that guided artificial cranial deformation, and other connected ideas about skull shape. Craniology is cringe-inducing when one considers the way that science has been perverted in the recent past to justify even the genocidal behaviour of colonisation, and the war-crimes that span out from it. Craniology is a great example of when science lacks emotional intelligence and self-reflection and is prostituted to help people forgive themselves for taking what they want.

In the realm of the skull more than anywhere else we get a taste of the ambiguous reactions with which our forebears viewed the appearance differences of our other ancestors, such as Neanderthals and Denisovans. In Mayan culture, Ancient Egypt, Central Asia, Austronesia, some parts of Africa, and Toulouse in France[1] — just to name some of the most evident examples — the shaping of the skull to have a long back of the head, and a sloping backward forehead is associated with beauty and prestige. Despite this fact the much-hated Cagot was described as having these features naturally and the impact of this difference for their people was a lot less empowering.

Numerous attempts have been made to try to explain where people in far-flung parts of the world got this particular idea that beauty looked like this. I think we must agree that whatever it was reached back a significant distance into history, much in the way the rule against pointing at rainbows does. At some point or another this head-shape had likely been witnessed, not just in one place but all over the world. In Toulouse, France,[2] where the image above derives from this artificial deformation of the skull was believed specifically to make you not noble and powerful, but wiser. The sloping back of the brow to make the forehead a less prevalent forehead, the larger occipital area, even the way the ears are taught to slope backward slightly by the angle of the skull, all brings about a resemblance to the Elder Folk. This is meditation-provoking. It makes it clear that Sapien attitudes towards the older peoples of the earth was mixed.

Witches are generally not considered a thing you want to look like. Yet in Toulouse this chosen form of deformation was associated with wisdom. Whereas in Egypt and South America it seems to have been connected more with nobility and perhaps even descent from the gods. Whatever we thought about the other human species that are also our ancestors it's clear that it was complicated and may have varied by location. Unlike Stan Gooch, who never got to assimilate the idea of

Denisovans into his Neanderthal theory, it is possible, almost certain, that Denisovans were significantly different culturally to Neanderthals.

This might seem obvious yet all too often we don't give enough time to simple observations like the fact that these people would have all had multiple complex cultures among them. Although the two species were more closely connected genetically than we are to either of them, like us they probably had different languages, different skin pigmentation depending on where in the world they were situated, and even nations among themselves, and that's before we even compare the two species to one another. Or perhaps it was the opposite, where there was no identification at all. Sometimes what we know we don't know is as important as what we do know.

The jewellery that has been discovered amongst a Denisovan DNA flavoured layer of the famous cave is far in advance of anything that Sapiens or Neanderthals were creating around the 70 000 years ago mark.[3] So, it's possible, given what we know about the concentration of Denisovan genes in current human populations that the ancestors of the Austronesian, Central Asian, South American, and maybe even the Huns primarily got their interest in this cranial shape based primarily on earlier Denisovan cultural success. Of course, I am not alone in making this leap, as authors such as Andrew Collins[4] have taken the proximity of the genes associated with autism to Denisovan DNA contributions as indicative that perhaps they were a kind of savant in the early human world.

Collins' work on Denisovans is a little like Gooch's was for the Neanderthals, something that makes bold leaps with the information available. It's his belief that the Animiki — belief figures of the Alonquian language groups whose name means thunderers or thunder-birds — were people of Denisovan origin. He then links this with the belief that certain families had the blood of the Animiki in their veins due to connections and even marriages with them. These gifted families were then seen as the source-river of the advanced mound building Adena culture.[5] If something even close to this is correct then one would expect to find the owners of their head shape held in high esteem indeed.

The author's suggestion is drawn primarily from the fact the Animiki were described as being able to take off their eagle form like a feather blanket or garment. As Neanderthal cave dust has been agitated of late and shown to contain traces of preserved skins of birds with dark feathers over in Europe, Collins takes this to suggest that perhaps Denisovans also used feather blankets in this manner. What I find far more compelling is that there is a form of feral mysticism that is said to derive from the Jes'sakkīd' who are a kind of wild shaman, separate in origin and function from the standard priest-driven Grand Medicine Society among the Ojibwa. The Jes'sakkīd' view their power as originating among the Animiki.[6] Whilst the Animiki don't seem to be despised as witches are, their outsider status suggests the aroma of the Elder Folk.

The use of a drill of some kind to make needles that take thread and bracelets indeed suggests the presence of a highly inventive people that may have been ahead of Sapiens. So we should not make the mistake of assuming the Denisovans to be less intelligent than ourselves, though, of course, different forms of intelligence also need to be considered. There is a sense of a different standing for the Elder Folk where Neanderthals dominated without as much Denisovan presence. The interest in shaping baby heads with artificial cranial deformation seems to be a bit different in Europe. The practice of cranial deformation was found amongst so-called peasants in France, rather than nobility, and perhaps not so connected with temporal power or royalty, as in other parts of the world. This is crucially important because we have no reason to assume that the Denisovans and the Neanderthals left us with one identical idea to rebel against, despite Collin's claim about Neanderthal use of feathers impacting the behaviour of Denisovans across the Atlantic. Or should we say copy, as well as rebel, or perhaps a mixture of both?

Judging from the large, worldwide collection of threatening ideas about menstrual blood, the left-hand, night-flying spirits, and covert cannibalism of all sorts, we can question, as Gooch did for Neanderthals, if perhaps the Denisovan lacked some of our key taboos, maybe even went as far as have a veneration around some (but maybe not all of) those same things? The far simpler explanation for crossovers in some areas is that Neanderthals also existed in Asia. At a glance one gets the feeling that although we can't prove Denisovans were a savant species they probably were more highly regarded by Sapiens than Neanderthals were. Places where artificial cranial deformation was associated with the gods and royalty are places where the so-called royals are more likely to have had contact with Denisovans and their descendants.

We can infer from some genetic similarities with Neanderthals that the skull shape[7] of Denisovans was not radically different from theirs. The Denisovan face was probably wider across the cheekbones[8] than that of your average Neanderthal or Sapiens. This means there's a great likelihood that the whole of the Sapien ancestral pool at one point met with someone, or most likely a culture or collection of cultures, that had this unusual sort of head, by comparison to our own. To me this is a possible explanation for why people would choose to artificially strap down and change their baby's head shape, especially in areas where that branch of Elder Folk might have been clearly more advanced than Sapiens at first meeting.

The matter is complicated somewhat by the fact that Neanderthals didn't just politely refuse to exist in Asia, Eastern Europe, or Australasia, but thrived there also. Nonetheless, the Easterly sources, who would have encountered Denisovans far more frequently than those further to the 'West', we come across this sense that this skull shape was a sign of nobility and to be sought after by purposely squashing the head of your infant until it yielded that form.

Of course, there were also exceptions to this in other parts of Asia where that face shape wasn't always an obvious compliment, such as the Witch (Layek) Queen Rangda from Bali. Rangda has very long teeth and like Layek is associated with cannibalistically devouring things including babies, she is connected with the colour red, and considered to be a force of chaos and destruction,[9] though when she's dealt with correctly she can also heal. There is a kind of ongoing competition between her and Bala-bala who is a part dog, part lion individual who inevitably overcomes her in the end. There is also the Polynesian goddess Hine-nui-te-pō another widow/woman of the Night figure, who discovers herself to be the victim of incest. Her description in her goddess of death form she takes after discovering her husband is her father, is one of obsidian teeth in both her vagina and mouth. Her eyes are like green stone, her hair like kelp and her mouth, significantly, sticks out like the teeth of a barracuda fish.[10] Both figures seem to be associated with the colour red and forces of chaos.

Another difference which might be significant in separating out Denisovan influence from that of Neanderthals is to be found in both Papua New Guinea, Australia, the Ojibwa Jes´sakkīd´ and South-East Asia more generally. In the Mekeo from Papua New Guinea allows for a male sorcerer who is publicly known and is a widower, called a 'man of sorrows', as the name ugauga must purify himself by fasting and sexual deprivation. Yet he steals the bodily secretions of women[11] to do his work, it is still worthy of our attention because it seems to point to a difference that might have something to do with the Denisovans and the areas they left their genetic imprint on the population most heavily.

When we approach the male witch or suangi, whose primary work seems to be a form of predatory cannibalism, we should take note of his tracks. A suangi is a type of male witch from a place where there is a strong genetic imprint of the Denisovan people (West Papua), one of the strongest ancestral traces in the world, and here the ritual of magical execution is associated with cannibalism in an overt way. Suangi are said to consume their victim from the inside, eating the blood and internal organs and stuffing the person up with leaves afterwards. The victim would go home zombified yet if they were able to name their oppressor before they died a few days later, then the family would not only kill but eat the supposed sorcerer to get revenge and take back the power. With the revenge cannibalism aspect we can see a similar practice as in described above in early German laws.

This is not the only cross-cultural example of this, in the fifth chapter of Burchard of Worms Corrector he put it this way in Germany during the 11th century:

[Have you believed] *while still in your body you go out through the closed doors... with others who are similarly deceived, and that without visible weapon you kill people... and cook and consume their flesh, and where the heart was you put straw or wood... and after eating these people you bring them alive again and grant them a brief spell of life.*

Whilst the motif of the cannibalised body filled up with straw or leaves that ends up dying in a few days is the same, the culprit in Germany is a woman, or a group of women in Burchard's work. All the way over to Arnhem Land in Australia there is a type of sorcerer who steals the blood from a victim, when their soul leaves their body the wound is covered and the victim appears to live for a day or two before expiring.[12] The main difference is that the German story involves night flight, and that it is explicitly done by women instead of men.[13]

The most intriguing space is South East Asia as a whole, where we see both the strongest concentration of surviving Denisovan DNA anywhere in the world, and also some of the largest amounts of Neanderthal genes to survive in any population. This makes it one of the hot-spots in trying to record the differing influences of the elder peoples on the taboo of witchcraft, and perhaps even separate out elements of difference between the two types of sorcerous footprints.

There are certain matters pertaining to the head or skull that we find strongly connected to witchcraft throughout the world. Worship of a head is found in witchcraft, often in relation to the First Dead or the veneration of Cain.[14] Worship of a head was included in the taboos supposedly broken by the Templars. We have already mentioned the Balinese Layek whose habit is to leave the body as a spectral head. This story is only one of the many similar witch stories of South East Asian countries, including Cambodia, Thailand, Indonesia, Singapore and Vietnam. Some of the material is startlingly familiar to anyone that knows much about Western European Witchcraft.

The most specific detail that links the ghost (but usually not just a ghost, often also the spirit of a living human that is sent forth while the owner sleeps) in this part of the world, is the notion of the severed head or disembodied head. This form is how the Layek appears when feeding, as a floating head with entrails and a corpse-light, that is often sighted as the witch's head uses it to find her way to her victim. The Krasue, as it is called in Thailand, possesses, similarly to the European witch, a spectral woman's shape. The primary difference is the shape of the spectre, which with the Krasue and Layek involves a disembodied head adorned with exposed internal organs.

The head is often viewed as being the seat of consciousness, though scientifically and magically speaking the gut is also part of our thinking body. This makes the Krasue a visceral embodiment of the consciousness of the witch. Though this is intriguing the reason that the gut is present in the Layek or Krasue is because they are hungry. Like most witches in a variety of nations, she is a feeder upon other humans. This sense of reciprocal paranoia, or fear of your own victim rising up in revenge, can be seen as a fear of hungry people fighting back against those who have food. In this way it links the South East Asian witch-figure with those who are oppressed and un-satiated.

As a person living in Tasmania, Australia, it is easy for me to imagine into this fear. One only has to remove history as we pass it down in our culture from your life. By this point, over one hundred and fifty years since the original people were being born and raised in their nations on country, the dominating culture would have conveniently forgotten a lot of the stories that talked about the horrors of The Black War, as it was called. We would likely know that someone else lived here before us, but without photographs, and original documents you can quickly imagine the Palawa and Pakana people having already begun to be mythologised, possibly even monsterised, even more so than they already were. Maybe by this time with no one talking about them much, and a selective history keeping, they would have started to appear to us as hungry…

Another thing that the disembodied head and tendrils of the South East Asian witch is reminiscent of is the entirety of the vagus nerve, simply hanging there in the air with a ghost-light around it. Images of a lone vagus nerve are very evocative of the Layek-shape. This is a little more than a mere visual similarity as the vagus nerve takes messages between the brain, heart, lungs, and digestive tract. Whatever aspects of Polyvagal Theory[15] we accept or reject it seems fair to say that this huge nerve is the primary intelligence of the vital functions in the body.

The business of being headless also rumbles into awareness for the student of the Western Occult Tradition in relation to the Bornless also called the 'Headless') Rite from the PGM (V.96–1721). In it we meet Akephalos, a deity not recognisable in either in Greek or Egyptian pantheons is clearly a divine being. Towards the end the invoking party switches from talking about Akephalos to speaking as him. Akephalos has this to say about himself:

I am the Headless Daimon with sight in my feet,
the Mighty One who possesses the immortal fire.
I am the Truth who hates the fact that unjust deeds are done in
the world.
I am the one who causes lightning and thunder.
I am the one whose sweat is the heavy rain which falls upon the
earth that it might be inseminated.
I am the one whose mouth burns completely.
I am the one who begets and creates.
I am the Favour of the Aiōn, my name is a heart encircled by a
serpent.
Come and follow.

Though the daimon could simply be seen as too old for a birth or beginning he is clearly literally headless as well, as he only has sight in his feet. Yet his head is likely still present in some capacity as his 'mouth burns completely.'[16] One certainly gets the feeling that perhaps the head and its absence, and paradoxical presence, is key to the power of the bornless one.

Notes

1. Amit Ayer, et al. The Sociopolitical History And Physiological Underpinnings Of Skull Deformation., Neurosurgical Focus, vol 29, no. 6, (2010), p. E1. Journal Of Neurosurgery Publishing Group (JNSPG), doi:10.3171/2010.9.focus10202 Accessed 19 Nov 2022.

2. Leila Galiay, et al. Intentional Craniofacial Remodelling In Europe In The XIXth Century: Quantitative Evidence Of Soft Tissue Modifications From Toulouse, France'., Journal Of Stomatology, Oral And Maxillofacial Surgery, vol 123, no. 5, (2022), pp. e342-e348. Elsevier BV, doi:10.1016/j.jormas.2022.05.002 Accessed 19 Nov 2022.

3. A.P. Derevianko, et al. A Palaeolithic bracelet from Denisova Cave., Archaeology, Ethnology And Anthropology Of Eurasia, vol 34, no. 2, 2008, pp. 13-25. https://www.academia.edu/69135303/A_Paleolithic_Bracelet_from_Denisova_Cave_?auto=citations&from=cover_page Accessed 19 Nov 2022.

4. Andrew Collins, The Coming of the Thunder People: Denisovan Hybrids, Shamanism and the American Genesis., Academia.

5. Andrew Collins, Ibid., p.10.

6. Collins, Ibid., p.10.

7. There are skulls we currently suspected of being Denisovan which may turn out to be proven to be later in this book's life-span. We have already a jaw-bone from Tibet that seems to confirm previous theories about the shape based on DNA.

8. Michael Price, Face of the Mysterious Denisovan Emerges., Science, Vol 365, no.6459

9. Michele Stevens, op cit., p.715.

10. Simone Peris, What Does Hine-Nui-Te-Po Look Like?: A Case Study Of Oral Tradition., Myth And Literature In Aotearoa New Zealand. (2022), p.1. https://search.

informit.org/doi/abs/10.3316/INFORMIT.498940776197408 Accessed 19 Nov 2022.

11.   Michele Stevens, op cit., p.718.

12.   A.P Elkin, op cit., p.121.

13.   In the sentences before the part I've quoted Burchard talks about the witch laying at her husband's bosom while her spirit fares forth.

14.   Andrew Chumbley's *Dragon Book of Essex* covers this topic.

15.   A theory relating to human stress response by Stephen Porges.

16.   Betz's translation of the PGM.

Chapter 11

Mirror Handed

When confronted with the image of our own reflection, whether in a shiny surface like volcanic glass, or in still water we are also greeted by a world in reverse. For this reason it is likely that the reflective nature of still water and obsidian were part of our ancestor's earliest and quintessential ideas about how to access the Otherworld. If we are right-handed, in that Otherworld on the reverse side of reality in the reflection we are left-handed. When you reach out with your right hand your reflection reaches out with their left. The natural tending direction for a left-hander who is blindfolded is to veer left when their eyes are covered, and a right hander veers to the right, giving each of us a lean.[1] Stan Gooch made this connection with the sinister history of the anti-left-hander bias, witchcraft, and the repressed ancestral memory of the Elder Folk, long before he could prove we were descended from the elder folk. Sadly he came to the conclusion it meant Neanderthals were probably primarily left-handers, which has since been suggested by evidence to be false. In reality they possessed the same right-handed bias Sapiens do.[2]

Our ancestors were able to perceive reflections in shallow water at the beach, in still water, or obsidian and other reflective stones. This second self must have appeared to be an even more empowered version of our physical shadow. Claude Lecouteux words it thus, including the images found in art beside reflections:

Shadow, reflection, image ensure the link of man to his fellow creatures, to the dead, and to the invisible world. Were this not the case, the examples given would remain inexplicable, and the shadow's oracular function would be, when all is said and done, merely a vulgar superstition.[3]

Our actual shadow is strongly associated with witchcraft and has numerous pieces of folklore attached to it, including ones that directly link it to luck, saying that to sweep over someone's shadow with a broom is to brush away some of their luck force. In former days a shadow wasn't a Jungian shadow, which in pop psychology has become a term for everything rejected by the super-ego, it was literally the actual place where light no longer falls because your body is in the way. It was a kind of powerful absence, a void of the self. The shadow of a witch was generally felt to be able to leave the body and be part of other people's nightmares.

If this rich folk-imaginal storytelling exists around a black patch cast because your existence came between light and ground, one can only imagine that the actual reflection of a person was just as impactful, if not more so. We see an extension of this in the way mirrors are treated as magical icons in superstition. Mirrors can be used to send away bad luck by reflecting the evil eye back at the source. To discover hidden treasures, or bewitchments concealed in the earth, a steel mirror will work against money troubles as it appears to double what you have.[4] One could peel an apple in front of the mirror to see the devil over the shoulder, or say one's own name three times with a candle in their hand to see the future.

Mirrors cannot be broken without terrible bad luck. If they are broken the shards must be washed under the moonlight, as if the moon has the ability to weave your luck-shreds back together. They must be covered during storms in case one catches the lightning in the house, and during the death of an occupant of the house then the most telling thing happens. At a death, to prevent the mirror's trapping the soul they must be covered over.[5] This probably reaches back to Otherworldly grimoire-invoked beings appearing in them during scrying. All of this make a lot of sense if our early ancestors first idea of another back-to-front version themselves was part of their first conception of a spirit world.

These early experiences of reflections and shadows were likely the heart of why the left-hand and back-to-front reality has come to be scorned and forbidden in nearly every country. In That Other Place the left is the hand the strange people, who are also the dead, use. With the left-hand taboo we are encountering another version of the rule against rainbow pointing, where something very similar is found all over the world, even among peoples who have not had contact with others for tens of thousands of years. In both cases it can be quite specific. That people are capable of holding onto taboos for this length of time shouldn't really be so surprising, given that Tasmanian Aboriginal people still told stories of when they could see icebergs in the sea near our island[6] which were melted through contact with the body of the moon goddess Vena, and considering icebergs were visible in the Last Glacial Maximus this is a true feat of information survival. There are also Aboriginal legends that tell of how the white swan became black, even though Aboriginal people haven't seen white swans since at least fifty-thousand years ago, and probably considerably longer.[7]

Cultures around the world from Iceland to South East Asia all place the left hand as sinister, in China there is extensive re-education to force right-handedness upon children.[8] In some parts of the Middle East the hand is considered dirty and used for ritually unclean actions.[9] A strong explanation for why this world-wide hatred for the left-hand must come from something more than the fact most of us are right-handed and the left-hand feels weaker for most, as, like some menstrual beliefs, it is very virulent. Somewhere in our very early history Sapiens came to associate the left-handedness of our reflections as the backwards state of another world, another world that one could hope to enter, or fear to enter, either in trance, dreams, or during death. It was a place where everything would be turned upside down.

In that world of the dead and the Other-place were taken to be in reverse. Language must be spoken backwards, things must move widdershins, people must look backwards through their legs when they want to see something marvellous or to curse someone, perhaps even at times foul was fair, and fair was foul in that place. Perhaps hairiness and holiness were connected there, as is reflected in numerous wild-man and wild-woman figures, and, of course, the primal facial structure given to the wicked witch.

If one takes this reversal idea further, in that other-side-world they are perhaps even hungry cannibal-spirits when, or even because, we are full. Those who are dead bide there, which might be anciently connected to why some cultures feel oddly about permanent images of the dead being preserved,[10] as the image becomes like a permanent link to the upside down version of their loved one.

The earliest record of religious persecution is that levelled at the Jewish people in the third century BCE in the writings of Manetho.[11] During this period accusations were thrown at members of this new monotheistic faith. They were accused of hating other people, of being unclean, and their refusal to eat pork was vilified. This led to a pogrom against them, one where they were forced to eat pork and some of them were burned to death. Whilst this hatred of the Jewish people has continued for the rest of recorded history and included their enslavement in Egypt, and the biblical story of the murder of the first born sons, there is still no proof available of these crimes.

When other religions and new cultures began to arrive they sought, as new religions tend to do, to suppress the presence of the older-way-of-seeing. To understand how they likely did this we can take Christianity as a model for what happens when a new religion, and in the older case even a new language. We know that Christianity began by trying to absorb things that were enjoyed by the people, such as holy wells and certain festivals, and later began forbidding things, whilst still allowing certain cross-overs to remain. From this we can get a model to understand what Maria Gimbutas's Old Europe might have been like, and how it likely yielded to outsider settlement that similar things might have happened. Somewhere between Otzi and his ten-percent Neanderthal genes and the present era we know something of genetic and cultural high impact happened in Europe and other Indo-European inhabited areas.

This, of course, doesn't stretch around enough of the world to explain the intense attitude towards the left-hand. It seems the stigma against the left is considered not to be as strong among either Indigenous Americans or the Arrernte people of central Australia.[12] The many peoples in Australia who were invaded in historical time had cultures that had complex societies with doctor men and women, and sorcerers who were cannibals, who flew at night. In some cases they considered women to have originally held primary spiritual power, but had it removed from them in the form of the aforementioned skirt, dilly-bag or bull-roarer. Sorcerers made agreements with dangerous powers, people placed taboos against menstruation, and sorcerers even stole children to cannibalise.

We also find among some particular Aboriginal cultures very strong taboos around menstrual blood that mimic those found elsewhere in the world. Given the large number of cultures on the Australian continent it is complicated, because in Australia there are also examples of circumcision rituals of boys that seem to mimic the bleeding of women, and the belief in some parts of Australia that the power women held was conferred by a skirt with women's blood on it. As we have heard, a dilly bag or skirt was stolen from the women at the beginning of time that meant that only men now had the powers that women had once kept for themselves. Other stories that I've heard told personally suggest that the first few women to enter Arnhem Land had very long clitoris', almost as if they were a dual-gender being, their organs seemed to be responsible for cutting in rivers and other features of the land. The men 'trimmed' them in some manner, which seems to mark the end of their full dreaming-spirit power.

In this we find the typical ambiguity towards the magic of women that is found in many other places in the world where Sapiens are settled, this idea that something is both powerful but requires inverting, needing to be repressed for some reason, one we may or may not know. Of course, this is all less simple than it appears, this example of using the reports of the beliefs of all Aboriginal Australians as an example of an uninterrupted culture due to the Pama-Nyungan language group accounts for 306 of the 400 Australian languages to pre-date British invasion.

This huge expansion of the language is only about five-thousand years old, about the same age as Otzi over in Europe. Whilst no major influx of blood-lines seems to have entered the genes of the population at that time, something of spiritual and social import must have happened, something that made the original bearers of the Pama-Nyungan language powerful enough to replace previous languages. It's difficult to say what it was, but there was certainly some kind of intense influence that came with it, and given that we are talking about a whole continent with numerous identities, and probably even more numerous languages, it's hard to say whether or not something could have changed from within during that time.

What we are left with though is that both the similarities and differences with the rest of the world's approach to and fear of sorcery suggests that the force Sapiens was trying to oppose and also ambiguously incorporate, was perhaps so old that even the Aboriginal nations had ancestors had met with the Elder Folk who carried those practices in their version of a dilly bag? This may have happened even before the various Aboriginal culture's incredibly long occupation of Country. Using the rainbow-pointing, the icebergs in the southern ocean, and the memory of white swans as examples of the longevity of cultural memory, we can travel deeper into understanding the taboos associated with witchcraft and sorcery. For whatever similarities one finds between Australian Aboriginal cultures and those on other continents must have been shared earlier than 50,000 to 70,000 years ago. The notion of witchcraft, what Emma Wilby, called dark shamanism when appears in the Amazon, is shaped by roughly the same features all over the world, with certain key, possibly systemic, differences.

Things are back-to-front in some way, just like in the reflections of this world in lucid surfaces. In Elkin's work we hear of an Aboriginal spirit doctor from Far Northern Queensland sacrifices an enemy man to his helper, cuts up his meat, puts aside his fat, and consumes him. Afterwards he cleans the bones and puts them together back to front. After this the man is believed to jump up again and live for three days before dying again.[13] Here we see the back-to-front assemblage of the bones, and familiar concept of being brought back to life for a short period of time before mysteriously expiring. We also see here the stealing of human fat to make special magically charged ointments with.[14]

The evil-eye is also a kind of backwards eye, where in Seidhr we find a lot of images of reversal and inversion, and the gaze as a form of dominance and dangerous intimacy. We are somewhere very familiar when we hear of the thrusting of skin bags or leather sack over a witch's head to prevent her from enchanting or cursing you, as we heard of above in early German sources. One also finds description of a seið-practitioner bending over and looking through their legs, often while grasping their earlobes when ready to cast or to break a spell, to 'turn the land upside down', or to invoke their own second sight. We see this clearly in the following example.

«What fiend is this coming towards us?" cried Högni. ' I can't make it out!' 'It's old Ljót on her way,' Þórsteinn answered, 'and what a tangle she's in!' She had cast her clothes up over her head and was walking backwards, and had thrust her head back between her legs; the look in her eyes was ugly as hell as she darted troll-like glances at them.[15]

If the left-handedness seen in our own mirror image was the first impression of an Otherworldly double, or shadow of the self, then it is also interesting to look at how the image of the handprint was one of the earliest worldwide representations of human presence. Handprints in ochre are common signs of Sapien presence from Africa, to Europe, to Australia. What we have learned recently is that Neanderthals did them before Sapiens arrived in Europe.[16] It is possibly noteworthy that the small finger is missing from the Neanderthal handprint image.

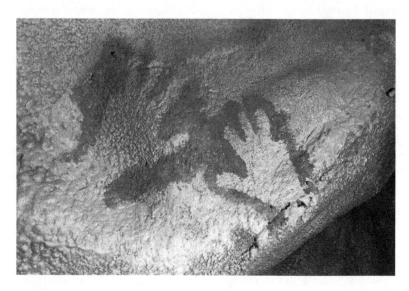

There are a number of Sapien cultures that practice the removal of parts of the little finger, including the Dharawal people of Southern Sydney, who take part of the little finger to turn people into a ghost-fisherwoman or man.[17]

The Neanderthal handprints are not thought to be the earliest found in the world, with that title going to Quesang, in the High Tibetan Plateau, dated to 226,000–169,000 years ago, these may belong to Denisovans.

The right hand stencils which are quite common may represent not only lateral convenience but the left handed reflection believed to be on the other side of the cave wall, where the ancestors might match their opposite hand to yours. The idea presented in The Mind in the Cave where David Lewis Williams talks about the artist's ability to free things from the Other Side through the wall of the cave after making multiple scratches across the surface during ritual, makes a lot of sense here. This idea hits deeper still with the suggestion that art arose fuelled from the idea that the reflection of something represents its Otherworldly self. That if you could make a detailed reflection, or shadow, of the animal you could tap into its Otherworldly nature, you could encourage it to sacrifice some of its spirit herd to the hunt, or perhaps just as importantly, to free some of its power to move among your people's collective fetch.

In European caves the multiple scratches over so many paintings and the layering upon layering, pictures drawn over other pictures frustrates the modern idea of a great painting. Yet this was a style that covered enormous distances in and includes to some extent the earliest painting believed to be done by the Elder Folk. If this does indeed turn out to be the work of Neanderthals then this cave art and those done by Sapiens is so obviously stylistically connected, and possibly even drawn by both species over a period of time, as one can see from the multiple dot work and the use of an item like a ladder, to allow an animal figure to exit the scene from above and then re-enter it from below. As it's been speculated that more than one painting session was involved in this unusual work, one must assume that there was not only a profane kiss but also an established connection in art-culture between the two peoples.

This seems to speak of a spiritual worldview that used art as a practical tool for spirit-working, and where the layering may have begun with painting already painted by Neanderthals. Not only were they perhaps seeking to create more prey animals as many have assumed, but to release a little of their essence into the cave so that it may be danced and sung with. In a world dominated by mega-fauna it isn't hard to see why these were the powers that humans looked to bring vitality to the group fetch. The connection between Sapiens and the fetch power of animals was well established and direct, and this potential layering of paintings suggests that the art culture between the Elder Folk and Sapiens may have been interactive. Did Sapiens find European caves already adorned? Here we must take a moment or two to meditate on the Underworld. It is likely that our cave painting forebears experienced a good deal of their spiritual experiences underground, sometimes in quite close relationship to difficult climbs down into the earth. As in Shadir where some Neanderthal humans were found who were killed during a cave-in we can assume these people all knew the danger they were facing in by climbing through tight passages into chambers where the oxygen levels are mind-falteringly low.

What draws my gaze is the fact that even as late as the coming of Christianity to Europe we still see examples of placing Hell below the ground. They weren't the only ones, Hade's realm is also away from the light and there is a tendency, whether in Nordic conception of the worlds, or in the hell-realms to be found in Buddhist and Hindu beliefs, for the Indo-European worldview to place what is considered superior above what is considered inferior. At an archeological level this could be seen as an almost literalist way of asserting the supremacy of the present day over the past that is buried lower.

There are memories of the previous cultures in stories such as those of the Vanir, who we have mentioned earlier in regards to their apparent brother-sister marriages. The Vanir were associated with orgiastic characteristics, flying through the air, were connected with elves and the Underworld, the terrifying witch-like art of Seidhr, and according to Clive Tully, were considerably to be favoured by women during rites of the home, which is just where you would expect the layover customs to retire to. The Vanir were overcome by the Aesir. It is interesting to note that during the war between the Aesir and the Vanir, Mimir whose name means 'the rememberer' is beheaded by the Aesir and so memory itself is lost.

Just as Bran is beheaded in the *Mabinogion* but still manages to continue to offer stories and wise counsel whilst his head kept alive, Odin preserves the head of Mimir and it continues to link him to Memory. This is likely a reference to the cult of the skull whereby memory can be conveyed via necromantic means and may remind us of the three days that those who are killed with sorcery are usually allowed to live on in a suspended state. This story seems to strongly hint at an attempt to interrupt the memory of a people, to oppose the ability of a culture to pass down its stories and customs.

The most important memory we have received of this earlier culture is that the use of Seidhr by the Vanir. Freya is burned for being too good at Seidhr, much like some other witches in various parts of the world, yet she regenerates each time. Seidhr is classed in written sources as something feminine and yet more powerful than other forms of magic. It results in Odin being told by Loki (who also had a history of turning into a woman and various animals):

But thou, say they, on Sáms Isle once
beat (the magic drum?) like a Vœlva:
in vitki's shape through the worlds didst fare:
in woman's shape, I ween.[18]

Other male practitioners were called things deemed worse than this such as 'tattered troll wench'. In the Helgi Lay there is an explicit association between the magical power of Seidhr and the back-to-front world's next favourite inversion after the back-to-front use of the sinister left-hand gender transformation. Diana L. Paxson words it like this:

Not only is the foe accused of having been a female, but a witch,
Valkyrie, troll-wench, or shape-shifter, specifically into the form of
a she-wolf or a mare (forms commonly associated with supernatural
or magical women), indicating a connection between transexuality
and spiritual power.[19]

The Norse sources probably do the best job of giving away the weird ambiguity with which such things were treated in a transformed Europe. It was at once both shameful to be ergi, or queer, particularly for the receptive party who was seen as being 'used like a woman', yet at the same time it was admitted that this rather back-to-front, rule-breaking, feminine oriented art was far more magically powerful than anything the new order could offer. It was so powerful that even Odin went on to master it, despite the shame accorded to men who used, or were used, by it.

Before the Indo-Europeans there was clearly a people whose religion was more aligned with older stories and older peoples. It was something earthward, associated with spinning and the distaff, possibly even leading to myths of flight on a distaff, downwards turning, working with the dead to achieve prophecy, back-to-front, deriving from women but passed to men, involving ecstatic trance states, gender inverting, shameful and yet also powerful, and perhaps even possessing some upside-down morality to the dominant culture. Perhaps this inversion took place through schismogenesis after the invasion? All of these things suggest that there was a holdover still present that harked back to a time when the Otherworld was first envisaged as being a bit like a reflection in still water or a polished stone, a world that favoured the back-to-front and the left-hand.

Notes

1. Christine Mohr, Test-Retest Stability Of An Experimental Measure Of Human Turning Behaviour In Right-Handers, Mixed-Handers, And Left-Handers., (2022). https://www.tandfonline.com/doi/abs/10.1080/13576500601051580 Accessed 20 Nov 2022.
2. Natalie T. Uomini, Handedness In Neanderthals., Neanderthal Lifeways, Subsistence And Technology, (2011), pp. 139-154. Springer Netherlands, doi:10.1007/978-94-007-0415-2_14 Accessed 21 Nov 2022.
3. Claude Lecouteux, *Witches, Werewolves and Fairies: Shapeshifters and Astral Doubles in the Middle Ages.*, Inner Traditions, (2003) p.146.
4. Eva Pócs, *Between the Living and the Dead: A Perspective on Witches and Seers in the Early Modern Age.*, Central European University Press, (1999) p.148.
5. Claude Lecouteux, op cit., p.146.
6. Helen F. Mckay, Gadi Mirrabooka: *Australian Aboriginal Tales from the Dreaming.*, Libraries Unlimited, (2001) p.39.
7. Donna Zaffino, The Dreamtime Story Of The Black Swan., Project GROW, 2019, https://projectgrow.com.au/blog/the-dreamtime-story-of-the-black-swan Accessed 21 Nov 2022.

8. Maura Elizabeth Cunningham, A Land Without Left-Handers., (2013), https://mauracunningham.org/2013/08/14/china-a-land-without-left-handers/ Accessed 21 Nov 2022.

9. Roxie M. Black, Cultural Considerations Of Hand Use., Journal Of Hand Therapy, vol 24, no. 2, 2011, pp. 104-111. Elsevier BV, doi:10.1016/j.jht.2010.09.067 Accessed 21 Nov 2022.

10. This feeling about displaying images of the dead is common among Australian Aboriginal people, for instance.

11. Miriam Pucci Ben Zeev, The Reliability Of Josephus Flavius: The Case Of Hecataeus' And Manetho's Accounts Of Jews And Judaism: Fifteen Years Of Contemporary Research (1974-1990) *)". Journal For The Study Of Judaism, vol 24, no. 2, 1993, pp. 215-234. Brill, doi:10.1163/157006393x00033 Accessed 21 Nov 2022.

12. Howard I Kushner, Retraining The King's Left Hand., The Lancet, vol 377, no. 9782, (2011), p.1 1998-1999. Elsevier BV, doi:10.1016/s0140-6736(11)60854-4 Accessed 21 Nov 2022.

13. Elkin, op cit., p.148.

14. Elkin, op cit., p.84.

15. Vatnsdœla Saga, ch 26, Searchworks. Stanford.Edu, 2022, https://searchworks.stanford.edu/view/80522 Accessed 23 Nov 2022.

16. Dahlia W. Zaidel, Paleoaesthetics: Evolutionary Studies In Imaginative Culture, vol 6, no. 1, (2022), pp. 143-146. Academic Studies Press, doi:10.26613/esic.6.1.291 Accessed 21 Nov 2022.

17. Les Bursill, Mary Jacobs, Dharawal Elder Aunty Beryl, Timbery-Beller, and Dharawal spokesperson Merv Ryan, Dharawal: The story of the Dharawal speaking people of Southern Sydney., p.20.

18. Loksenna, pp.23-24.

19. Sex, Status, and Seiðr: Homosexuality and Germanic Religion Originally published in Idunna 31, 1997 Sex, Status, and Seidh: Homosexuality and Germanic Religion by Diana L. Paxson.

Chapter 12

Hollow Riding Voices

We have met the Layek and the Krasue, who should actually be referred to as Phi Krasue[1] she is a woman who appears as a floating-head-witch. Though the influence of European ideas about vampires has changed her to someone seeking mainly human blood, originally her connection was very much to human filth. Both herself and the male version, the Krahang, were attracted via the presence of filth and likely to enter people via the anus. Taboo violation in magical practice led to one becoming one of these creatures. Though the office was also hereditary, much like some European witchcraft, and could be passed between people via the sharing of saliva[2] — another inhuman kiss.

The Krasue's male counterpart, the Phi Krahang, is also a sorcerer who finds his way to his nature through taboo violation. He engages in similar night-flying behaviour, but is, or in some cases was, a human man, an outsider who is partly an insider, by day. Much like that of the Krasue he is a Person of the Outside, he even uses a sak tam khao, a rice winnowing pole to fly by night, much as the European witch is associated with mounting the broomstick or distaff pole.

He is considered to be the husband of the Phi Krasue, so there may be an example here of contagious witchcraft, especially as we know that sharing saliva can lead to infection.

The main difference between the two exists in form, something with the exposed entrails is almost always a woman — witch. The entrails are also highly important, appearing as either the focus for the need to consume filth, commit cannibalism, or as the actual impetus to enact a form of human predation involving life-force.

Seeing the example of the riding of the sak tam khao draws our attention to a certain pattern. Something which conveyed power to the bearer during daily life, usually a humble tool is used as the mount for a night flight. If you go back far enough into the past rice winnowing poles, winnowing bowls, and brooms wouldn't have been so humble at all, but a symbol of ultimate power over one's environment. We can imagine the broom as having a very ancient history, possibly a simple wooden, highly biodegradable brush of this sort was one of the tools that may predate Sapiens and been used to clean many a cave or campsite.

A distaff, another riding tool of the witch, also has this distinction of being an item not thought much of today that would once have been the backbone of an entire industry, and had connected its own set of mysteries. Women's industries where spinning and weaving allowed a great deal of financial independence existed in many cultures. Once again the association between women and weaving appears to be old enough that it predates the nations of Europe as they now stand. The association between Seidhr, the Norse form of witchcraft, with spinning and weaving is one of the main reasons it was shamed as a primal woman's art, as we will see more of below.

This is not the only example where items that gave people power in society where used as mounts during sky flight. Baba Yaga rode around in a mortar wielding a pestle, something that points to both the poisoner's and the healer's art, using the mortar as a wand. In most cases though the riding item went between the legs in some way as if one were riding it like a horse. Jordanes de Bergamo. In his *Quaestio de Strigis* of 1470,[3] Bergamo writes of witches who on 'certain days or nights they anoint a staff and ride on it to the appointed place or anoint themselves under the arms and in other hairy places...or they [push the ointment] under their nails, the mouth, ear, or under their hairy areas or underarms.' The mention of nails, mouth, and ear somewhat detracts from the sexual interpretation commonly given to broom riding.

Earlier than this we think we know that Irish witch Alice Kyteler[4] had a closet where they found ointment, which she apparently greased her riding pole with, and ambled around the room with it between her legs. However, it turns out this detail wasn't added until a long time after her trial. Whilst applying flying ointment to an area that would readily absorb it is certainly part of the mounted stance the fact it is ridden seems more important here, much in the way one would mount a horse, and what the item is has seldom been explored at a symbolic level. Strange items of all sorts including chairs and stoves are ridden by witches in some parts of the world.[5]

Usually the item is something that confers power on the person, or something in the past associated with power, for cooking or even for sitting, given that even chairs have not always belonged to everyone. The distaff which we find Frigga riding in a twelfth century mural in a cathedral in Germany was once a prime item of women's empowerment. Later on we see Albrecht Durer repeating this theme with his hag witch riding a distaff. The one of the earliest art depictions of witches riding brooms is of Waldensian heretics being portrayed as witches. One of them rides a broom the other a long white pole that looks a bit like a staff.[6]

The guts of this idea is that the witch must ride something when she flies, whether it be another entity, like a horse or a wolf, or a symbolic entity that represents power and stepping over a barrier or hedge. At other times it is another person who she rides, as in hag-riding. Sometimes it is the sorcerer themselves who is ridden by spirits. In this riding narrative we can better understand the prohibitions against male practice of Seidhr, a form of Norse sorcery which had feminine connotations. Just as the Witch of Endor endured her encounter with the dead to no ill-effect yet Saul was depleted, witchcraft was seen as different for women and men in much of Europe.

Seidhr could include the act of being penetrated by spirits — making the man ergi or unmanly in Norse culture, for he too had been 'ridden'. This process of riding someone in the role of nightmare, known as hag-riding, and being ridden by spirits seems to be part of the mythos underpinning the mounted witch. A link between spinning and weaving and moon phases is clear due to prohibitions about spinning in the moonlight. Marie Trevelyan's recorded that women were forbidden to spin in the moonlight lest they make a hangman's noose for someone.[7]

The Fates, of course, are depicted as spinning and cutting thread. Seidhr was also connected with weaving, probably because this activity involved potential sorcery to influence Fate. Though it doesn't appear like one on the surface many nations depict the moon as a spider, who is also a talented spinning animal. Spider Woman in Hopi and Navajo attached a thread of spider silk to each person while the world was created so they could stay in contact with her.[8] Both spinning and spiders seem to be connected with the moon in various cultures where spinning and weaving are almost universally a woman's mystery.

The Pawnees of North America actually call the moon the spider woman. The Paresi of Central Brazil also identify the moon as a spider. The Indians of the Banks Island in Canada say the companion of the moon god, and his associate in the creation of mankind, is a spider. In far off Borneo the moon is deity is said to have assumed the form of a spider and spinning a web. Among the Nias of Indonesia the soul of the moon is a spider. In the Loyalty Islands of Melanesia the spider and the worm are representatives of spirits that send rain, and all water is seen as connected to the moon.[9]

It is perhaps also important to note that the spider lays down a cross followed by a widdershins spiral, turning leftward, when she first begins her work, something which is very evocative of the witch's use of a crossroads and an anti-clockwise spiral. Someone who moves among the subtle world might also notice that the very basis of reality can feel like it is constructed of threads. As an initiate from the Lower Murray area (Yaralde) in

Australia put it when describing the experience of the postulant during his making:

Do not be frightened. If you get up you won't see these scenes, but when you lie down again you will see them, unless you get too frightened. If you do you will break the web [or thread] on which the scenes are hung.[10]

This is quite common symbolism in the magic of Australian Aboriginal sorcery where the clever rope that is inserted into the body during a Making, is taken out to ride, or to lift one's self to the heavens. At one point Elkin describes the use of this rope for the clever man as being used 'like a spider uses its thread' to get around in the spirit world.[11] Whether this life-poetry begins with the sense that the world was created of subtle threads like a spider's web, or with women being the ones to spin and weave, and then the moon became associated with the activity due to the twenty-eight day cycle of menstruation, is unclear. Like a spider's web it is hard to see where the starting point is. What is clear is that the moon, women spinning and weaving and spiders are all intimately connected. There is a subterranean, ancient link between these things that is no doubt older than the diffusion of Sapiens across the world, for the connection with weaving and women exists in locations as far flung as Polynesian and Australian Aboriginal cultures.

One of the terms used for a Seidhr practitioner was hamhleypa, 'hamingja-leaper, shape- or skin-changer'. Given that witch's-shirt was a term for clothing made using weaving-magic and designed to protect the wearer, it seems possible that this kind of 'skin changing' or outer covering changing that, sorcerous women engaged in was connected to this textiles magic, as much as it was to spectral transformation into an animal during flight. Someone who could spin and then weave a magical warding garment was indeed acting as a skin-changer.

Burchard of Worms (965-1025)[12] asserted indeed that it was the Fates, those turners of thread, who could change a man into a werewolf, and, of course, as mentioned above in Wales it was the woven girdle that gave a witch the power of the Fates over man who crossed a threshold. The Fate women masquerading as midwives could also decide whether a child born with a caul was to be what different type of stigoi or seer.[13] This makes it clear that when we are punishing these malefactors the recipient of correction was also believed to have no choice about their nature as a magical individual. Neanderthal people seem to have paved the way when it comes to woven rope so we should not make the mistake of thinking that this kind of binding-threads magic was unique to Sapiens.[14]

The spae-wife had a pole that she may have hit the mat with to create a beat whilst going into a trance, one that could relate to the plain white pole the Waldensian woman was shown to ride. The practice of climbing up a pole to sit higher than the rest of the room or perhaps on a platform may relate to the practice of Finnish sorcerers who were known to be able to change into a variety of creatures to fly to other locations and also ascended when doing certain types of work. In this sense the climbing of the pole is adjacent to the act of flying on one, and we will later encounter parallels to this when it comes to Aboriginal clever rope.

Other than items of power witches rode animals. The spirit-woman of the nightmare is often known to come riding not on a mare but on a wolf.

The woman did what she said she would do and around midnight she saw a small, old neighbour woman riding a wolf and saw her enter through the closed door. As the old woman approached [her previously harmed child's] cradle, the mother put the burning iron

on her face. The old woman left, emitting a great cry. The next
morning the mother went to the woman's house with some bailiffs
and arrested the woman who indeed had a mark on her face.[15]

Freya was also depicted riding a boar, and Frau Holle riding a swan. One feels that this is connected to transformation into the animal, as a way of expressing the borrowing of that animal's vital force by the witch or spirit. The animals painted into the cave walls of the underground art temples of our Palaeolithic forebears may have had a similar potency when danced with under low oxygen conditions, especially if an entheogen was also being ridden.

Sometimes these arts of flight also involved projectiles, which were an extension of this idea of sending something through space with magical intent. This again may have its roots in spear throwing sorcery from old hunting charms. Often the magical arts of the Finnish sorcerers (Lapps) included magical archery,[16] that made you unable to miss a target, being able to shoot three arrows simultaneously with magic arrows which fly back to the bowstring of their own accord and hit whatever they are shot at. This archery magic is also recorded as practiced by male witches in Reginald Scot's *Discovery of Witchcraft*,[17] where arrows are shot into statues of Christ by archer witches who are also unable to miss. These archery feats cannot help but remind us of Robin Hood.

These stories of projectile magic all have something in common with the stead of the witch on which the sorcerer is able to send themselves through space. This archery magic makes us think also of elf-shot, common in European folklore, where the elves, or witches like Isobel Gowdie who went riding with The Good Folk, were said to shoot stone-tipped arrows to harm livestock and people. There are also benevolent uses of arrows in the San dance where arrows of N/om or power, where both power and sickness can appear as an arrow.[18]

Like many impulses that come through witches there is a sense that the world of the wild, the Underworld, and the buried head of Memory must try to take back something for itself. Some items, like the N/om arrows or the clever rope are actually inserted into the body during initiation, which means the process is often experienced as violent. Men of high degree in the Lower Murray area were put through all manner of psychic terrors during their initiations including multiple stabbings and having their insides taken out.[19]

Cave paintings from Europe abound of men with multiple spears put through them in what is likely an image of an initiation, where sharp objects being driven into the body by spirits to put them through a death before their death. Such things are also experienced during initiation in Tibet.[20] The strange thing about the forces worked with here is that their intrusion can result either in death or inspiration, and some situations involving both, depending on how prepared the individual is for the experience.

What we can untangle from the traces of these ancient woven mats, and ghosts of ochre on stone, is that witches both ride and are ridden. The magical technology of this is much like that of whispering a horse into compliance. There are a few things that are required to whisper an animal into obedience, one is an unerring sense of relaxed self-confidence, one that teaches the fetch of the other animal that they have some unknown reason to respect you, and maybe even fear your gentle but relaxed form of self-assertion.

This quality may be passed down in families and augmented with tricks passed from teacher to student. Whispering lineages follow lines where something is extra warm in their fetch and the red-serpent of their bloodline. They come with a certain expertise that allows the person to manipulate the creature with scents and signals, but all in all if ego gets in the way you can be sure the animal smells it far before Sapien animals do. A single moment of self, or animal, doubt and you are lost. In a similar way witches may ride swans and even wolves, but you cannot get up on them through thinking you are better than them, only through realising you are part of them, and they of you.

In a similar way brooms, distaffs, and winnowing poles are symbols of a power. From an animistic perspective they are people just like animals are, they possess their own Virtues and powers, namely the ones that allow them to get their job done. In folklore brooms allow you to clear a space, but they are also very connected with acquiring and collecting luck, and sweeping away the luck or influence of others. Distaffs and spindles connect us to the Fates, and how early that association began is difficult to say, yet despite often being hard physical laborious work from Ancient Egypt, to the Philippines and as far as Arnhem land weaving is known at the spiritual domain of women. This makes one suspect that weaving might have been a woman's mystery even as far back as Africa, where all our Sapien ancestors form a source-river.[21] Or maybe this link goes back even further, to something to do with spiders and the moon and women that has an even more ancient source.

Even if the original pole ridden by a witch was a distaff in Europe the fact the sak tam khao, or rice winnowing pole, was used by the witch-like sorcerer of Thai tradition suggests there is no original item of greater significance than the others. The pole could be a spear, an arrow, a broom, a distaff, a winnowing pole, a mortar, a staff, or a clever rope. It might lift you higher than a bird, or plunge you down int the earth like a goanna[22], or shoot you through the air, powered by the animistic qualities of that item. Those qualities seem to be shaped by what that tool brings to the human world. Whatever it is it has something to do with power that is not over one's environment but in it, whether that be cleaning, weaving, cursing or healing.

Whatever the powers of these different types of poles we may imagine they take their inspiration from the bones of things — with bones representing the fundamental truth behind the existence of something. Though they are unlikely to be physically hollow like a bone they channel voices and messages from another place, they send intent there too when projected. These little elf-darts of consciousness help us to cut holes in reality and step through an entrance that is guarded by the one who watches the threshold, so that we may make a bold assay. Just as Gwydion stole the pigs of Annwn, and Prometheus the fire of the gods, they represent relocations of certain powers from the Underworld that the witch or sorcerer continues to wield, that may even end up integrated into their body.

In many Aboriginal cultures based around what we now call in Victoria and inland New South Wales, coastal and inland Queensland the rod or broom for a sorcerer becomes a cord or a pointing bone. Here we are able to learn a little more about why I might compare the staffs of witches to hollow bones, things have to be spiritually hollow if they are to echo forth voices. The first Elder Folk person to make a musical instrument out of a hollow bone would have discovered this.

In many different parts of Australia cord or rope which takes the place of a broom, probably not much different to what the Elder Folk were making, is put into the postulant's body at initiation, a practice that seems to range across large areas. The sorcerer can take the cord out to climb up to the sky or use it to shoot negative or positive influences and items into people, or move around on it like spider silk. Like the quartz crystals that are also inserted into the body in some cultures at initiation these cords become like part of the flesh. Whilst they can be extracted they are a little like the extra bone, something often believed to belong to the Hungarian Taltos figure and to remove their power if taken.[23]

The Taltos is one of those magical figures that clearly predates Christianity yet is often absorbed very easily into a world of saints, and church-tinted magic. The extra bone belonging to the Taltos, who can be either male or female, is the source of their sacred power, though they usually also manifest with a caul at birth. Sometimes that extra bone took the form of a sixth finger.[24] When one Taltos was accused of being a witch and asked the difference between a Taltos and a witch, she replied that a Taltos is fighting for Hungary in heaven. Naturally it was not learned it was instead weaved that way.

This placing of sanctity in a fleshly manifest form, as part of the human body helps us to get a better understanding of sorcerous cannibalism. It is believed that this kind of sacred cannibalism was very prevalent among Australian sorcerers in some parts of the continent. Interestingly there are many parallels between the way magical power is passed between sorcerers in Australia as they are passed between holy men in Tibet — both places with a strong Denisovan genetic signature. Just as in the bone of the Taltos, the blood, kidney fat, and ground down bones of both clever and holy men in Australia, the Aghora we spoke of earlier, and in some Tibetan practice ingest parts of the human body during the Making of new experts. Blood is drunk and fat is procured from the bodies of Clever Men which creates an immediate power increase for the sorcerer who receives it, opening doors into the sky.

This initiatory motif can be found in Europe as well where we hear about Patak Nógrád country in 1759 both the removal of a bone from someone and another victim being 'torn to pieces' at the top of a tree and told they had to keep their dismemberment a secret. Others describe being devoured upon entry to their spirit dreams. In Australia sometimes their important hole in the sky was guarded by the ghost of a woman, or figures described as goddesses, which occasionally seems to reinforce the idea of the art having its beginning with women. Another spirit-doctor was able to do this by chewing on a piece of cured stomach skin he had cut from the woman when she died. When he would chew this skin the door would open for him.[25] This places me in mind of the relentless skin chewing associated with the clothing manufacture of the Elder Peoples, whose teeth show this evidence of spending a lot of time chewing leather. One wonders if this was also a meditative practice as well as part of clothing manufacture?

Given how often parts of the body of the practitioner were eaten as an entry point into magic one could say that the body of the deceased Man of High Degree is ridden through its very ingestion up to the sky world[26] to meet with new helpers just as the skin of the woman helped this sorcerer to fly upon chewing. We also find bamboo used instead of clever rope or string, a type of material which is hollow in nature. More often than not it is string, or clever rope, that takes the place of the broom or winnowing pole among Aboriginal doctors of the spirit. This is ridden to the sky which becomes open to reveal the realm of ghosts, but there are also bones, and occasionally hollow bamboo used to suck spirits into their navel.[27]

There is a string also used in Hungarian sources we hear of Mihaly Csordos who describes certain women had given him the string for healing and taught him to recognise bewitchment.[28] Some Aboriginal sorcerers are also known for various forms of pointing the bone, this is usually over-simplified in popular understanding. Much like the cord, this bone seems to be taken from inside the human body. It is a human bone, connected by human hair or possum twine to a receptacle made of a human shinbone, or arm bone, and it is used among other things to draw blood from a distance, and to send influence across space.

Whilst some of the more nefarious Australian practices sound easily as unpleasant as those of witches in Europe the attitude towards sorcery, which is primarily a male concern on this continent, seems to be far more mixed than in most parts of the world. Even spirit-practitioners, men of high degree, who have many skills in common with a witch seem to be respected or at the very least feared and very seldom purged. In fact, people who are culturally-tuned in this manner will die very quickly if they are sung or have something pointed at them. This fact allows us to understand the power of magic more deeply.

Chapter Six of *Aboriginal Men of High Degree* talks about the way people from traditional groups are impacted by being sung. Many of them received what is classed as 'white fella magic' from medical doctors to no good effect. Unless what Elkin calls a medicine man could suck something out of their bodies they believed was there, or otherwise clear them of influence, they would continue to pine even whilst otherwise 'healthy'. What was discovered is that a cure for a medical condition they were facing would help a white person, but not an Aboriginal person who had been sung. They seemed to need to receive a spiritual salvation as well.

The spirit doctor was considered to be the real saviour when things went right. What this tells us is that there are various channels through which magical healing and harm can pass in a person. Something about the action of belief, what some might call faith and others knowing, moves through the body of the person and catalyst and changes something, reorganising them. It would be less likely that a singing would work on someone who doesn't have that knowing. It seems that the magic stones, quartz crystals, clever rope, extra bones, and various other materials inserted into people's bodies during initiation and healing have the effect of anchoring the sorcery of belief? Perhaps this is why in Patak Nógrád a bone, probably something that was fixing into place the faith in the old system is removed from the body during initiation?

Christians have been inclined to see faith as a virtue of sorts, yet a simple understanding of something in science we know as the placebo effect can take us far beyond the warm fuzzy feeling of faith. Knowing the reality of something gives that thing power over you, and it also gives you power over other things. We may begin to see the tools of the sorcerer in this regard, as items that represent something that exists as a power within their body, as entry points via which preternatural influences can gain ingress and turn the threads of fate around. Just as we have read above where Catholicism was supposedly able to be removed from the body of the heretic after ingesting saliva from a familiar of their new persuasion, faith exists, in a magical sense as something as tangible as an extra bone in the body, as rope, as teeth, as quartz crystal. And as the clever string and the quartz crystal used to sing or heal someone was stored inside the body of the medicine man, so the item being ridden is an extension of the truth-stored-in-flesh, the interior powers of that sorcerer, which can even be ingested after that person's death.

Notes

1. The term 'phi' designates a kind of spirit that practices magic. See: Benjamin Baumann, Phi Krasue: Inhuman Kiss (Mongkolsiri, 2019) Monsters, Peter Lang, p.106.

2. Baumann, Ibid., p.106.

3. M. Harner, The role of hallucinogenic plants in European witchcraft. In M. Harner (Ed.), *Hallucinogens and shamanism*. New York: Oxford University Press.

4. Tom Hatsis, Those Goddamn Ointments: Four Histories., Journal Of Psychedelic Studies, vol 3, no. 2, 2019, pp. 164-178. Akademiai Kiado Zrt., doi:10.1556/2054.2019.025 Accessed 22 Nov 2022.

5. Hatsis, Ibid., 164.

6. Éva Pócs and Gábor Klaniczay, Communicating with Spirits., Central European University Press, (2005) pp.160-162.

7. Marie Trevelyan, op cit.

8. Lynne Wilcox. Grandmother Spider: Connecting All Things. Preventing Chronic Disease, vol 4, no. 1, 2007, p.1., https://www.ncbi.nlm.nih.gov/pmc/articles/PMC1832128/ Accessed 22 Nov 2022.

9. Stan Gooch, op cit., p.1087.

10. Elkin, op cit., p.61.

11. Elkin, op cit., p.88.

12. Lecouteux., op cit., p.110.

13. Pócs., op cit., p.88.

14. Rick Doble, The Development of Advanced Woven-Fiber Technology in the Paleolithic Era., p.9, https://deconstructingtime.blogspot.com/

15. Etienne de Bourdon, Septum Doni spiritus sancta, no. 364, Paris 1940 319-21

16. Viking Answer Lady Webpage, Women And Magic In The Sagas: Seidr And Sp". ch. V, Vikinganswerlady.Com, 2022, http://www.vikinganswerlady.com/seidhr.shtml Accessed 23 Nov 2022.

17. Reginald Scot, The Discoverie Of Witchcraft, p.37, Google Books, 2022, https://books.google.com.au/books?hl=en&lr=&id=oWN84aaURhwC&oi=fnd&pg=PR18&dq=Reginald+Scot+The+discoverie+of+witchcraft+archery&ots=1qKK61xIzh&sig=7Zbkn1uuba9-K-83rQcP_vFig6Q&redir_esc=y#v=onepage&q=archery&f=false Accessed 23 Nov 2022.

18. Low, Chris. The role of the body in Kalahari San Healing Dances. Hunter Gatherer Research. 1. pp.29-60. (2015) / hgr.2015.3. p.36.

19. Elkin, op cit., p.60.

20. Elkin, Ibid.

21. Carol P. Christ, Weaving the Fabric of Our Lives, Journal of Feminist Studies in Religion, vol. 13, no. 1, 1997, pp. 131–36. JSTOR, http://www.jstor.org/stable/25002303 Accessed 23 Nov. 2022.

22. Elkin, op cit, pp 150-151.

23. Eva Pócs, Between the Living and the Dead, op cit., p.140.

24. Éva Pócs, The Hungarian Táltos and the Shamanism of Pagan Hungarians. Questions and hypotheses., In: Acta Ethnographica Hungarica 63, 1 (2018): 149-196 Accessed May 9, 2022 https://doi.org/10.1556/022.2018.63.1.9

25. Elkin, Ibid., p.84.

26. Elkin, Ibid., p.49.

27. Elkin, Ibid., p.149.

28. Pócs, op cit., p.152.

Chapter 13

Dropping into Radial Castle

There are at least three different core stories that form the web of spirituality and magic practice all around the world. All of them are intermingled with Sapiens, but there are two other fore-parent paths, that of the Elder Folk usually called Neanderthals, and that of the more easterly based elder race — known as the Denisovans. It is subtle, but if you put your ear to their ancient graves, to be found inside our own bones and blood, we can hear the faint echoes of their differences to each other, and to the purely Sapien ancestors who originated in Africa.

Naturally with the weight of all this time built up there are only hints that we are able to hear through research. The sense that perhaps the Denisovans were once more highly regarded than the Neanderthals, due to the beliefs that formed around cranial deformation and nobility in the areas they lived? There is also a sense that the Elder People of Europe, with their proven use of woven thread[1] had something to do with the connection between women and weaving. Though it is difficult to prove one also gets the sense that Neanderthals may have held more in common with Bonobos when it comes to flexible sexual patterns, gender relations, and perhaps experienced less aversions to their own body than many Sapiens do.

The notion of the moon as a spider is more concentrated in areas with a higher percentage of surviving Denisovan blood. Mystical cannibalism on the other hand seems to have been connected with the rites of all types of sorcery from Neanderthal caves, to Sapiens in Tibet, and the certain absence of Denisovan fossils despite their genetic diversity could point to the practice of ritual cannibalism. Whether or not these species that make hybrids of us were more invested in the practice than us, it certainly seems there is a belief among Sapiens that eating other people, even if you are trying to absorb their clever fat or their body parts, makes people in some way less human.

There are whispers also that the notion of women as the source blood — though not the limitation — of what we now call witches is more of a Neanderthal legacy than a Denisovan one. As the areas where we find the greatest concentration of Denisovan genes are the places where sorcerers were either just as likely to be men, or were equally as likely to be men. It is likely we owe the notion of the old woman witch with the long teeth to Neanderthal forebears, and that they were credited more with being wise rather than noble. It is possible, though, of course, hardly provable as yet, that Denisovan people were once a bit ahead of Sapiens when it came to manufacturing complex jewellery and tools, and that Neanderthals created art before Sapiens arrived in Europe.

The other difference is one of trajectory. Sapiens with higher amounts of Denisovan blood seem to share the rest of our species preoccupation with the rigorous control of menstruation, and the door they use to enter the spirit world is more often located in the sky than under the earth. The teaching ancestors seem to come from the stars, especially the Milky Way, and share a large spiritual emphasis on The Pleiades. Whereas the focus is more on the Underworld in the areas which were Neanderthals did not share that space with Denisovans is undeniable. Whilst in all societies there are evil sorcerers who are suspect of causing trouble, the gender of those people is more often either equally male and female, or more likely to be male in Denisovan occupied places.

As we have explored in the previous chapter there seem to be belief-crystals, special bones, or faith activated clever-rope, that our bodies come to hold over time as sorcerers. These are built up of lore, experience, inserted by initiating teachers or spirits, and often also intuitively impactful forms of proof. Those substances are also promoted by our ancestors, and sometimes also forebears who still live in the substance of Country, who hold certain doors open for us, whether that door be in the sky, or into a stone lined chamber full of bones. For some of us certain types of gateways are more likely to be held open than others.

Of course, every so-called Sapien is a mixture of all of these ancestors, doors, lands and talents, with certain things rising in each generation and each time someone is deemed cunning or clever enough for this Art. What this means is that the idea of race, this concept that we are ancestrally marked in some definitive way, because of what country we were born in or our skin-tone is to sadly oversimplify things. Each cunning person is a mysterious eruption of magic. It pays to remember that even those of us whose have done DNA tests and know themselves, as I do, to possess the blood of the Elder Folk, but not explicitly the Denisovans, that Neanderthal people had also interbred with the Denisovans before they met us.[2]

There is probably no Sapien alive that doesn't contain this triplicity at the very least. Every time a Marked person is born a fate wheel is spun, or a Fate-woman decides what ancestor and what beast will guard our doorway to the Otherwise. How then should we step out in spirit with a full knowing not just in our brain but anchored into our flesh? The guts and viscera of this path is to be found in the poetry that holds it. We must go out into the moonlight over months of waxing and waning, and whilst we do engage in nothing but feeling into the weave of the spider's web behind the appearance of things. We must begin with sitting out, as it was called in Nordic sources, or deep listening (dadirri), as some Aboriginal people call this state of sensory openness. This will alert the one who holds our door that we are ready and alert enough to connect with the Elder Folk that live on inside us. In this reverse extinction event we call them forth, whether their knowledge was in the earliest weaving of cord, or in moving around via the constellations of the stars, or both, we cut a door for them with our attention, just as they will cut one for us. It is even better if we can do this kind of sitting out far from the noise and lights of Sapien dwellings. Do not use any words, especially if you wish to connect with the Neanderthal forebears. Instead make non-verbal humming, hissing, or wordless song to them to come forth, as you pull out the thread of the spider inside your own bones to link it to the web of things so you can climb.

You will know when the time is right to sally forth on that subtle structure. Explore its shape with your hands, you may find you have many hands. Do so many times before you attempt to find the places where many of these threads meet up. Make a habit of learning things with your body, with touch instead of sight. Notice what changes as the moon and seasons change. While you are out there you should wait for a hunger to drive you. Don't try to rush it. Interference of the will or feeling fear is usually going to break the thread that holds the vision together. You need to be patient. Feel out the embroidery of reality's backdrop until you get a sense that something needs you.

Perhaps you will be met by an ancestor. Do not expect to see them necessarily. They may present as a voice or as a purely tactile presence. Getting out of the Sapien-specific obsession with vision and appearance is important to connecting with the web. From here you can ward yourself and your property by generating and moving around thread. You can journey to other people and check them over for intrusions, suck things out, wrap them up, discard them, drain off power from the refuse. There is also the ability to draw sheen and fat off from places that have too much of it. Afterwards you can consume it to power yourself up for an important act of magic, or you can gift it to others, not necessarily human others, who have less of it than they need, or store it in a tool. If you should wish to take something from a place of excess it is important that you learn how to make transparent thread, to make yourself as clear as crystal, to obscure your red desires until you have assumed the condition, and therefore the appearance, of the dead.

In nearly every culture that has clever people, cunning ones, sorcerers, there is some sort of initiation that helps you to die before you die. The brutality of the spirits in forming and shaping you will pay off later because you will find yourself able to strip away the sentimentality of life, the attachment to this particular form you appear to have, that lies sleeping at home while you travel, it will allow you to open yourself to passing off as other creatures, of hiding behind different forms. In this way you are unlikely to be recognised when you travel the threads. Before you can obtain this though you will pass, either if you haven't already or just additionally, through some sort of trauma of making, an initiation. Fear and pain will be involved. The reason for this is that you seek to move without obstruction from normal mortal limitations, and so you will be leaned on until you learn to be flexible in the many little hands of the Fate-spiders.

You may wish to obtain a physical object in which to store Virtue that you gather in your missions. Whatever tradition or culture you are chosen by, in the form of ancestor helpers will determine whether you object is a black stone of obsidian or jet, a quartz stone or perhaps even a spool of rough twine around a blackthorn rod. This will help you to store or move around illnesses and disease as well as Virtue. The method for removing things that trouble others is exactly the same as moving around the fat, you must simply learn to clear yourself of it without sentiment or attachment at the end, otherwise sickness will follow you in ways you do not intend.

Learn to listen to the voices of the Older People, those wants and needs that are not always a spoken voice but could come to you from any part of your body. Your body is the holy-of-holies because without it you would not be able to hear the voices of the lost ancestors who we have only remembered with our conscious minds recently. All of your body speaks. It is both tabernacle and divinatory tool. If you use a bone or a distaff you must think of them as taken out from your own body. The distaff is the part that can weave, just as a spider can weave from inside its own body. The broom is the part that knows how to clean and collect and discard.

Regular time spent in deep-listening will give you the talents you need to become a master worker of the threads. You will also develop deeper than normal empathy for others that can be activated and toned down at will. You should not be a victim of it only a wielder of it. This can be used to develop forms of sensual and sexual ecstasy when the right people who can meet you there are available. When they are not you will find there are spirits who are like a twin of yours, people with an opposite hand they use in the mirror, people who will teach you ecstasy, and we will in turn teach it to them. There is no Person of the Outside who is able to work the threads who will not in time conjure people of flesh and people of subtle flesh, known to some as spirits, who can answer the ancestor-driven desires we are lit up by. None of us who are part of the living cosmos are truly made to be alone.

Notes

1. Rick Doble, op cit., p.9.
2. John Hawks, Neanderthals and Denisovans as biological invaders., PNAS, Vol. 114 | No. 37, August 31, (2017).

Bibliography

Anaar, Originally published in *Witch Eye*, Volume 10, Divine Twins, the dual divine force of the Feri Tradition, (2022). Retrieved 14 November 2022, from http://feritradition.org/grimoire/deities/divine_twins.html

Apuleius; Ellen D Finkelpearl. (Trans.) (2021) *The Golden Ass* (edited and abridged by Peter Singer). New York: Liveright Publishing Corporation; London.

Ayer, et al. *The Sociopolitical History And Physiological Underpinnings Of Skull Deformation.*, Neurosurgical Focus, vol 29, no. 6, (2010), p. E1. Journal Of Neurosurgery Publishing Group (JNSPG), doi:10.3171/2010.9.focus10202 Accessed 19 Nov 2022.

Bello, et al, *Upper Palaeolithic ritualistic cannibalism at Gough's Cave* (Somerset, UK): The human remains from head to toe. Journal Of Human Evolution, 82, (2015) pp.170-189. doi: 10.1016/j.jhevol.2015.02.016

Benedict, *Patterns of Culture.*, Houghton Mifflin, (2005).

Black, *Cultural Considerations Of Hand Use.*, Journal Of Hand Therapy, vol 24, no. 2, 2011, pp. 104-111. Elsevier BV, doi:10.1016/j.jht.2010.09.067 Accessed 21 Nov 2022.

Blust, *Pointing, Rainbows, and the Archaeology of Mind.*, Anthropos. 116. (2021) 10.5771/0257-9774-2021-1-145.

Bourdon, *Septum Doni Spiritus Sancta,* no. 364, Paris (1940).

Bovin, *Nomads Who Cultivate Beauty: Wodaabe Dances and Visual Arts in Niger.*, The Nordic Africa Institute (2001).

Bower, H Sivers, *Cognitive Impact of Traumatic Events.*, Development and Psychopathology vol. 10,4 (1998): pp.625-53. doi:10.1017/s0954579498001795

Brewer, *Jaguars and slaves: European constructions of cannibalism in colonial Latin America* – ProQuest. (2022), p.23. Retrieved 13 November 2022, from https://www.proquest.com/openview/

fba87f57ee2f14c1eb809839ab44a506/1?pq-origsite=
gscholar&cbl=18750

Brunet, *Bridging The Transgenerational Gap With Epigenetic Memory.* Trends In Genetics, vol 29, no. 3, (2013) Elsevier BV, doi:10.1016/j.tig.2012.12.008 Accessed 19 Nov 2022.

Bursill, Mary Jacobs, Dharawal Elder Aunty Beryl, Timbery-Beller, and Dharawal spokesperson Merv Ryan, *Dharawal: The story of the Dharawal speaking people of Southern Sydney.*

Cabarrouy, *'The Cagots, Excluded and cursed from the southern lands'.* J. & D. éditions. (1995).

Carbonell et al, *Cannibalism as a Paleoeconomic System in the European Lower Pleistocene: The Case of Level TD6 of Gran Dolina* (Sierra de Atapuerca, Burgos, Spain) | Current Anthropology: Vol 51, No 4. (2022). Current Anthropology. Retrieved from https://www.journals.uchicago.edu/doi/abs/10.1086/653807

Christ, *Weaving the Fabric of Our Lives*, Journal of Feminist Studies in Religion, vol. 13, no. 1, (1997) JSTOR, http://www.jstor.org/stable/25002303 Accessed 23 Nov. 2022.

Clay, *Female Bonobos Use Copulation Calls As Social Signals.,* Biology Letters. (2022), https://royalsocietypublishing.org/doi/abs/10.1098/rsbl.2010.1227 Accessed 19 Nov 2022.

Cohn, *Europe's Inner Demons: The Demonization of Christians in Medieval Christendom.,* University of Chicago Press; Revised ed. edition (2001).

Collins, *The Coming of the Thunder People: Denisovan Hybrids,* Shamanism and the American Genesis., Academia, (2018).

Conde-Valverde, Mercedes et al. *Neanderthals And Homo Sapiens Had Similar Auditory And Speech Capacities.* Nature Ecology &Amp; Evolution, vol 5, no. 5, 2021, Springer Science And Business Media LLC, doi:10.1038/s41559-021-01391-6 Accessed 24 Nov 2022.

Cudmore, agus ag ól a fola: *Ingesting Blood and Engendering Lament in Medieval Irish Literature.* (2021) Brill, pp.165-189. Retrieved from https://brill.com/display/book/9789004499690/ BP000019.xml

Culotta, *Neanderthals Were Cannibals, Bones Show,* Science Vol 286, no.5437,pp.18-19

Cunningham, *A Land Without Left-Handers.,* (2013), https://mauracunningham.org/2013/08/14/china-a-land-without-left-handers/ Accessed 21 Nov 2022.

Darmetester, *The Zend-avesta,* Oxford, (1880).

Derevianko, et al. *A Palaeolithic bracelet from Denisova Cave.,* Archaeology, Ethnology And Anthropology Of Eurasia, vol 34, no. 2, (2008). https://www.academia.edu/69135303/A_Paleolithic_Bracelet_from_Denisova_Cave_?auto=citations &from=cover_page Accessed 19 Nov 2022.

Doble, *The Development of Advanced Woven-Fiber Technology in the Paleolithic Era.,* https://deconstructingtime.blogspot.com/

Eliade, Birth and Rebirth: *The Religious Meaning of Initiation in Human Cultures,* Harper and Brothers, New York, (1958).

English Standard Version Bible, *1 Samuel 28.* (2001). ESV Online. https://esv.literalword.com/

Frazer, *The Golden Bough: A Study in Magic and Realism,* a New Abridgement from the Second and Third Editions. New York: Oxford UP, (1994).

Galdikas, *National Geographic-157* (1980).

Galiay, et al. *Intentional Craniofacial Remodelling In Europe In The XIXth Century: Quantitative Evidence Of Soft Tissue Modifications From Toulouse, France'.,* Journal Of Stomatology, Oral And Maxillofacial Surgery, vol 123, no. 5, (2022) Elsevier BV, doi:10.1016/j.jormas.2022.05.002 Accessed 19 Nov 2022.

Gallop, *The Book of the Basques.,* University of Nevada Press, (1970).

Gerald of Wales, *Vision of Britain,* Book 1: Usk and Caerleon. (2021). Retrieved 25 December 2021, from https://www.visionofbritain.org.uk/traveller

Ginzburg, Ecstasies: *Deciphering the Witches' Sabbath.*, The University of Chicago Press, (1991).

Graeber and Wengrow, *The Dawn of Everything: A New History of Humanity.*, Farrar, Straus and Giroux, (2021).

Gregory IX *Bull Vox* in Rama.

Gregory MD, et al, *Neanderthal-Derived Genetic Variation Shapes Modern Human Cranium and Brain.* Sci Rep. (2017) Jul 24;7(1):6308. doi: 10.1038/s41598-017-06587-0. PMID: 28740249; PMCID: PMC5524936

Guy, *Humiliation: A Theme in Ecclesiastical Folklore.* (2022) Retrieved 13 November 2022, from https://www.proquest.com/openview/271bf49582fc2e99eccf9d13e1d76761/1?pq-ori gsite=gscholar&cbl=2026366&diss=y

Haak, Wolfgang et al, *Massive Migration From The Steppe Is A Source For Indo-European Languages In Europe.* Cold Spring Harbor Laboratory, (2015) doi:10.1101/013433 Accessed 19 Nov 2022.

Hald, *What Types of Pornography Do People Use and Do They Cluster? Assessing Types and Categories of Pornography Consumption in a Large-Scale Online Sample.* The Journal Of Sex Research. (2022) Retrieved from https://www.tandfonline.com/doi/abs/10.1080/00224499.2015.1065953

Hanham, *The Scottish Hecate: a wild witch chase,* Scottish Studies, (1969).

Harner, *The role of hallucinogenic plants in European witchcraft.* In M. Harner (Ed.), Hallucinogens and shamanism. New York: Oxford University Press, (1973.)

Harris, *George MacDonald's Frightening Female: Menopause and Makemnoit in The Light Princess.*, 12 November 2022, from https://digitalcommons.snc.edu/cgi/viewcontent.cgi?article=1205&context=northwind

Hatsis, *Those Goddamn Ointments: Four Histories.*, Journal Of Psychedelic Studies, vol 3, no. 2, (2019) Akademiai Kiado Zrt., doi:10.1556/2054.2019.025 Accessed 22 Nov 2022.

Hawkins, Chimeras that degrade humanity: the cagots and discrimination., Academia Paper, (2014)

Hawks, *Neanderthals and Denisovans as biological invaders.*, PNAS, Vol. 114 | No. 37, August 31, (2017).

Henderson, *Survival in Belief Amongst Celts*, James MacLehose, Glasgow, (1911).

Hoffmann, et al, *The dating of carbonate crusts reveals Neandertal origin of Iberian Cave Art.* Science, 359, 6378

Hollox, Luciana W. Zuccherato, *Genome Structural Variation in Human Evolution.*, Trends in Genetics, (2021) https://doi.org/10.1016/j.tig.2021.06.015

Hopkins, *The Discovery of Witches: In Answer to Several Queries.*, Witches of the Atlantic World: A Historical Reader and Primary Sourcebook. Ed. Elaine G. Breslaw. New York, (2000). pp.37-41.

Howel, *Contemporising Custom: the re-imagining of the Mari Lwyd* – Research Repository. (2022). Retrieved 14 November 2022, from https://eprints.glos.ac.uk/5861/

Ihobe, *Male-male relationships among wild bonobos (Pan paniscus) at Wamba, Republic of Zaire.* Primates 33, (1992). https://doi.org/10.1007/BF02382747

Inbar, et al, *Disgust Sensitivity, Political Conservatism, and Voting.*, Social Psychological and Personality Science, 3(5), (2012) https://doi.org/10.1177/1948550611429024

Ivanhoe, Erik Trinkaus, *On Cranial Deformation in Shanidar 1 and 5* | Current Anthropology: Vol 24, No 1. (2022). Current Anthropology. Retrieved from https://www.journals.uchicago.edu/doi/abs/10.1086/202956?journalCode=ca

Khan, *Ötzi – more Neandertal than the average bear.* (2022). Retrieved 14 November 2022, from https://www.discovermagazine.com/health/otzi-more-neandertal-than-the-average-bear

Kirk, *The Secret Commonwealth of Elves, Fauns and Fairies.*, Dover Publications, (1933)

Kushner, *Retraining The King's Left Hand.*, The Lancet, vol 377, no. 9782, (2011) 1998-1999. Elsevier BV, doi:10.1016/s0140-6736(11)60854-4 Accessed 21 Nov 2022.

Kutz I, *Revisiting the lot of the first incestuous family: the biblical origins of shifting the blame on to female family members.* BMJ (Clinical research ed.), 331(7531), (2005) https://doi.org/10.1136/bmj.331.7531.1507

Larena, et al, *Philippine Ayta possess the highest level of Denisovan ancestry in the world.* Current Biology, 31(19), (2021) 4219-4230.e10. doi: 10.1016/j.cub.2021.07.022

Lecouteux, *Witches, Werewolves and Fairies: Shapeshifters and Astral Doubles in the Middle Ages.*, Inner Traditions, (2003).

Listova, *A Program for Collection of Material on the Customs and Rituals Associated with Childbirth,* Soviet Anthropology and Archeology, (1999) 30:2, DOI: 10.2753/AAE1061-1959300253

Low, *The role of the body in Kalahari San Healing Dances.* Hunter Gatherer Research. 1. (2015) /hgr.2015.3. p.36

Map, *De Nugis Curialium of ~1180*

Marris, *Neanderthal Artists Made Oldest-Known Cave Paintings.*, Nature, (2018), https://www.nature.com/articles/d41586-018-02357-8 Accessed 19 Nov 2022.

Martin, *The History Of Witchcraft,* Google Books, (2022), https://books.google.com.au/books Accessed 2 Nov 2022, p.32.

May, *Why is Incest Porn So Popular?* https://www.vice.com/en/article/8gdz8k/why-is-incest-porn-so-popular-332

McArthur, E., Rinker, D., & Capra, J. *Quantifying the contribution of Neanderthal introgression to the heritability of complex traits.* 'Nature Communications', 12(1). (2021) doi: 10.1038/s41467-021-24582-y

McGowan, *Eating People: accusations of cannibalism among second century Christians.*,

McIntyre, et al. *Bonobos Have A More Human-Like Second-To-Fourth Finger Length Ratio (2D:4D) Than Chimpanzees: A Hypothesized Indication Of Lower Prenatal Androgens.*, Journal

Of Human Evolution, vol 56, no. 4, (2009) Elsevier BV, doi:10.1016/j.jhevol.2008.12.004 Accessed 19 Nov 2022.

Mckay, Gadi Mirrabooka: *Australian Aboriginal Tales from the Dreaming.*, Libraries Unlimited, (2001).

Mohamed, K. Durrant, C. Hugget, J. Davis, A. Macintyre, & S. Menu, et al. *A qualitative exploration of menstruation-related restrictive practices in Fiji, Solomon Islands and Papua New Guinea.* (2018) ONE, 13(12), p.1, e0208224. doi: 10.1371/journal.pone.0208224

Mohr, *Test-Retest Stability Of An Experimental Measure Of Human Turning Behaviour In Right-Handers, Mixed-Handers, And Left-Handers.*, (2022), https://www.tandfonline.com/doi/abs/10.1080/13576500601051580 Accessed 20 Nov 2022.

Montgomery, *A Cross-Cultural Study of Menstruation, Menstrual Taboos, and Related Social Variables.*, Ethos Vol. 2, No. 2 (Summer, 1974) Montgomery.

O'Donovan, *Irish Sagas: Echtra mac nEchach Muigmedóin text.* (2022) Retrieved 14 November 2022, from https://iso.ucc.ie/Echtra-mac/Echtra-mac-text.html

O'Shea, *The Perfect Heresy: The Revolutionary Life and Death of the Medieval Cathars.*, New York: Walker & Company, (2000) pp.80-81.

Ott, '*Impure Blood: The Menstrual Taboo in the Christian Church During the Thirteenth Century*', St. Mary's Academy2021). Retrieved 25 December 2021, from https://pdxscholar.library.pdx.edu/cgi/viewcontent.cgi?article=1143&context=young historians

Paxson, *Sex, Status, and Seiðr: Homosexuality and Germanic Religion.*, Originally published in Idunna 31, 1997 Sex, Status, and Seidh: Homosexuality and Germanic Religion

Peris, *What Does Hine-Nui-Te-Po Look Like? A Case Study Of Oral Tradition.*, *Myth And Literature In Aotearoa New Zealand.*, (2022), p.1. https://search.informit.org/doi/abs/10.3316/INFORMIT.498940776197408 Accessed 19 Nov 2022.

Pfuhl, & L. Ekblad, *Neurodiversity traits linked to Neanderthal Admixture.*, (2018) https://doi.org/10.31219/osf.io/w4nh5

Pócs and Gábor Klaniczay, *Communicating with Spirits.*, Central European University Press, (2005)

Pócs, *Between the Living and the Dead: A Perspective on Witches and Seers in the Early Modern Age.*, Central European University Press, (1999) p.148.

Pócs, *Hungarian Táltos and the Shamanism of Pagan Hungarians. Questions and hypotheses.*, In: Acta Ethnographica Hungarica 63, 1 (2018): 149-196 Accessed May 9, 2022 https://doi.org/10.1556/022.2018.63.1.9

Price, *Face of the Mysterious Denisovan Emerges.*, Science, Vol 365, no.6459

Radke, et al, *Purifying selection on noncoding deletions of human regulatory loci detected using their cellular pleiotropy*, Genome Research, 31, 6, (935-946), (2021).

Ríos, et al. *Skeletal Anomalies in The Neandertal Family of El Sidrón (Spain) Support A Role of Inbreeding in Neandertal Extinction.* Sci Rep 9, 1697 (2019). https://doi.org/10.1038/s41598-019-38571-1

Roach, *Roots of Desire: the myth, meaning and sexual power of red hair.*, Bloomsbury Publishing, (2005).

Robb, (2007). *The Discovery of France: a historical geography from the Revolution to the First World War.* New York London: W.W. Norton & Company.

Rolleston, *Myth and Legend of the Celtic Race*, T.Y Crowell, New York (1911).

Rosenberg, *High-pitched voice theory – Neanderthal* – BBC science, https://youtu.be/o589CAu73UM

Russell, *Magic Mountains, Milky Seas, Dragon Slayers, and Other Zoroastrian Archetypes.* Bulletin of the Asia Institute, 22, pp.57–77. http://www.jstor.org/stable/24049235

Scot, *The Discoverie Of Witchcraft*, Google Books, 2022, https://books.google.com.au/books?hl=en&lr=&id=oWN84aaURhw

C&oi=fnd&pg=PR18&dq=Reginald+Scot+The+discoverie+of+
witchcraft+archery&ots=1qKK61xIzh&sig=7Zbkn1uuba9-K-
83rQcP_vFig6Q&redir_esc=y#v=onepage&q=archery&f=false
Accessed 23 Nov 2022.

Scott, *Minstrelsy of the Scottish Border Consisting of Historical and Romantic Ballads, collected in southern counties of Scotland; with a few of modern date founded upon local tradition.*, Project Gutenberg eBook. (2021). cxiv 24 December 2021, from https://www.gutenberg.org/files/12742/12742-h/12742-h.htm

Scott, William Henry Barangay, *Sixteenth-century Philippine Culture and Society.* Ateneo University Press, (1994).

Shreeve, *The Neandertal Enigma: Solving the mystery of human origins.*, Penguin Books, (1997).

Skov, & S. Peyrégne, et al. *Genetic insights into the social organization of Neanderthals.*, Nature 610, pp. 519–525 (2022). https://doi.org/10.1038/s41586-022-05283-y

Soper, Echoing Retorts in Hárbarðsljóð and Lokasenna. Scandinavian Studies 94(4), (2022) pp.475-503. https://www.muse.jhu.edu/article/869134.

Svoboda, *Aghora: At the Left Hand of God.*, Sadhana Publishing, (1998)

Stephen, *Witchcraft, Grief, and the Ambivalence of Emotions,* American Ethnologist. (1999) 26 (3): doi:10.1525/ae.1999.26.3.711. JSTOR 647444

Stoneking, *Widespread prehistoric human cannibalism: easier to swallow?* Trends In Ecology & Evolution, 18(10), (2003) pp.489-490. doi: 10.1016/s0169-5347(03)00215-5

Tablet 8, The Epic of Gilgamesh.

Straubhaar, *Nasty, Brutish, and Large: Cultural Difference and Otherness in the Figuration of the Trollwomen of the "Fornaldar sögur"*, Scandinavian Studies 73, No. 2 (Summer 2001)

Tan, et al, *Bonobos respond prosocially toward members of other groups.*, Sci Rep 7, 14733 (2017). https://doi.org/10.1038/s41598-017-15320-w

The Sampradaya Sun – Independent Vaisnava News – Feature Stories. July 2006. (2022). Retrieved 14 November 2022, from https://www.harekrsna.com/sun/features/07-06/features360.htm

Thiessen, *The Social Construction of Gender. Female Cannibalism in Papua New Guinea.*, Anthropos, Bd.96, H.1 (2001), pp.141-142.

Trevelyan, *Folklore and Folk-Stories of Wales.*, chapter 16, Retrieved 14 November 2022, from https://www.amazon.com.au/Folklore-Stories-Wales-Marie-Trevelyan/dp/0854099387

Turk, Matija et al. *The Mousterian Musical Instrument From The Divje Babe I Cave (Slovenia): Arguments On The Material Evidence For Neanderthal Musical Behaviour.*, L'anthropologie, vol 122, no. 4, (2018) Elsevier BV, doi:10.1016/j.anthro.2018.10.001 Accessed 24 Nov 2022.

Uomini, *Handedness In Neanderthals.*, Neanderthal Lifeways, Subsistence And Technology, (2011), pp. 139-154. Springer Netherlands, doi:10.1007/978-94-007-0415-2_14 Accessed 21 Nov 2022.

Vatnsdœla Saga, ch 26, Searchworks. Stanford.Edu, 2022, https://searchworks.stanford.edu/view/80522 Accessed 23 Nov 2022.

Viking Answer Lady Webpage, *Women And Magic In The Sagas: Seidr And Spellcraft.* ch. V, Vikinganswerlady.Com, (2022) http://www.vikinganswerlady.com/seidhr.shtml Accessed 23 Nov 2022.

Weyrauch, *Gypsy Law: Romani Legal Traditions and Culture*, University of California Press, 13 Aug 2001.

Weyrich, L., Duchene, S., Soubrier, J. et al. *Neanderthal behaviour, diet, and disease inferred from ancient DNA in dental calculus.* Nature 544, 357–361 (2017). https://doi.org/10.1038/nature21674

Wilby, *The Visions of Isobel Gowdie: Magic, Witchcraft and Dark-Shamanism in Seventeenth century Scotland,* Sussex Academic Press, (2010).

Wilcox, *Grandmother Spider: Connecting All Things. Preventing Chronic Disease,* vol 4, no. 1, (2007) p.1., https://www.ncbi. nlm.nih.gov/pmc/articles/PMC1832128/ Accessed 22 Nov 2022.

Wilde, *Ancient Legends, Mystic Charms and Superstition.,* Boston, Ticknor and co. (1887).

Wolf, *Cultural Conceptualizations of Magical Practices Related to Menstrual Blood in a Transhistorical and Transcontinental Perspective.,* Cultural-Linguistic Explorations into Spirituality, Emotionality, and Society, (2021) chapter: 14.

Zaffino, *The Dreamtime Story Of The Black Swan.,* Project GROW, 2019, https://projectgrow.com.au/blog/the-dreamtime-story-of-the-black-swan Accessed 21 Nov 2022.

Zaidel, *Paleoaesthetics: Evolutionary Studies In Imaginative Culture,* vol 6, no. 1, (2022) Academic Studies Press, doi:10.26613/ esic.6.1.291 Accessed 21 Nov 2022.

Zeev, *The Reliability Of Josephus Flavius: The Case Of Hecataeus' And Manetho's Accounts Of Jews And Judaism: Fifteen Years Of Contemporary Research (1974-1990)*Journal For The Study Of Judaism, vol 24, no. 2, (1993) Brill, doi:10.1163/157006393x00033 Accessed 21 Nov 2022. [Original source: https://studycrumb. com/alphabetizer]

About the Author

Lee Morgan lives on a communal covenstead on kunanyi/Mt Wellington near Nipaluna/Hobart, where he creates sanctuary for other weirdos, and raises books, people, and ideas from the grave. He has had novels and non-fiction published by Moon Books, Three Hands Press, Witches Almanac and Rebel Satori. Having survived an enormous meningioma, Lee currently is busy filling the room in his skull with new brains, writing Folk Horror, and queering the world one step at a time. You can find his website which will lead to blogs and books at: leemorganbooks.com

Witchcraft books by the author include

A Deed Without a Name:
Unearthing the Legacy of Traditional Witchcraft

The field of witchcraft studies is continually over-turning new information and research about traditional witchcraft practices and their meanings. *A Deed Without a Name* seeks to weave together some of this cutting-edge research with insider information and practical know-how. Utilising his own decades of experience in witchcraft Lee Morgan pulls together information from trial records, folklore and modern testimonials to deepen our understanding of the ecstatic and visionary substrata of Traditional Witchcraft.

Standing and Not Falling:
A Sorcerous Primer in Thirteen Moons

The Otherworld is ready for you, but are you ready for the Otherworld? What would you tell your own less-experienced self about magic if you could go back in time and make a better start? That is the question this book seeks to address. What might you need to slough off, how far might you need to walk from the comfortable and familiar to truly embrace a magical life? Covering a period of thirteen moons, *Standing and Not Falling* is a workbook that allows the reader to clear the way before embarking, or to conduct a spiritual detox on themselves before stepping up their practice, or engaging a new beginning.

Sounds of Infinity:
Traditional Witchcraft and the Faerie Faith

This story about faerie began as a vision. In his newest work, Lee Morgan follows a cacophony of visions with sharp, bright edges to them that have lain claim to his heart and hands. In what is clearly a work of the heart, Lee explores and then bypasses rational intellect guiding the reader to experience the touch, scent, and feel, of the Faerie Faith through symbol and suggestion.

The Gusty Deep

The Gusty Deep is an epic monster-tale that pokes holes between world ages and lets them chatter to one another through a keyhole in the moss. In this very adult faerie-tale, twelfth-century Britain descends into the chaos of The Anarchy. Lux, daughter of the surviving member of the Green Children of Woolpit, narrowly escapes a forced marriage with a stranger, with the help of a way-faring man named Robin Goodfellow. He takes Lux back to his band of Others — the queer, the whores, and the witches — together, can they save the land, its resources, and their very right to exist as the world slips into civil war?

MOON BOOKS
PAGANISM & SHAMANISM

What is Paganism? A religion, a spirituality, an alternative belief system, nature worship? You can fi nd support for all these definitions (and many more) in dictionaries, encyclopaedias, and text books of religion, but subscribe to any one and the truth will evade you. Above all Paganism is a creative pursuit, an encounter with reality, an exploration of meaning and an expression of the soul. Druids, Heathens, Wiccans and others, all contribute their insights and literary riches to the Pagan tradition. Moon Books invites you to begin or to deepen your own encounter, right here, right now.

If you have enjoyed this book, why not tell other readers by posting a review on your preferred book site.

Readers of ebooks can buy or view any of these bestsellers by clicking on the live link in the title. Most titles are published in paperback and as an ebook. Paperbacks are available in traditional bookshops. Both print and ebook formats are available online.

Find more titles and sign up to our readers' newsletter http://www.johnhuntpublishing.com/paganism

For video content, author interviews and more, please subscribe to our YouTube channel.

MoonBooksPublishing

Follow us on social media for book news, promotions and more:

Facebook: Moon Books Publishing

Instagram: @moonbooksjhp

Twitter: @MoonBooksJHP

Tik Tok: @moonbooksjhp

NOTES

NOTES